FIRED EARTH
1000 YEARS OF TILES
IN EUROPE

A SCARBOROUGH ART GALLERY TOURING EXHIBITION

RICHARD DENNIS PUBLICATIONS

TILES & ARCHITECTURAL CERAMICS SOCIETY

Catalogue
Editors: Hans van Lemmen and John Malam
Design: Hilary Edwards-Malam
Photography: R A Simpson Photographic Studios
Production: Wendy Wort
Typesetting: Alphabet Studio
Printing: Flaydemouse, Yeovil

Exhibition
Organizer: Josie Montgomery, Scarborough Art Gallery
Sponsors: Scarborough Borough Council,
   Fired Earth Tiles plc and the Museums & Galleries Commission
Designers: Haley Sharpe Associates, Leicester

Published in Great Britain by:
Richard Dennis Publications
The Old Chapel
Shepton Beauchamp
Somerset TA19 0LE

Enquiries about the Tiles & Architectural Ceramics Society should be addressed to:
Hans van Lemmen
Faculty of Cultural & Education Studies
Leeds Polytechnic
City Campus
Leeds LS1 3HE

ISBN 0-903685-28-0

A catalogue record for this book is available from the British Library

FIRED EARTH

CONTENTS

ACKNOWLEDGEMENTS

Many people have helped towards this exhibition becoming a reality, and I wish to offer my special thanks to the following individuals who have lent material or who have given it their active encouragement and support. The roll of honour is:

Peggy Angus
Valerie Baynton
Ken Beaulah
Frances Beresford
Chris Blanchett
Carlo Briscoe
Myra Brown
John Burgess
Alan Caiger-Smith
Jon Catleugh
John Challener
Ann Clark
Kenneth Clark
Helene Curtis
Chris Dellow
Richard Dennis
Angela Drakakis-Smith
Edward Dunn
Leslie Durbin
Hilary Edwards-Malam
Albert Gallichan
Alan Garlick
Diana Hall
Anne Harris
Elizabeth Hartley

Richard Henriques
Paul Henry
Tony Herbert
Kathy Huggins
Louise Irvine
Joan Jones
Elspeth King
Nicholas Kneale
Hans van Lemmen
Gesine Mahoney
John Malam
Lynne Moore
John Morris
Hilary Myers
Richard Myers
Jan O'Highway
Shaun Ormrod
Peter Rose
Karen Rowe
John Rumsby
John Scott
Colin Simpson
Mike Sixsmith
Debbie Skinner
Jeremy Southern
Robert Tate
Matt Townsend
Sally Veall
Bronwyn Williams-Ellis
Jonathan Waights
Karin Walton

The following institutions and organizations have kindly lent material and support:

Bristol Museum & Art Gallery
The De Morgan Foundation
The Doulton Museum
Fired Earth Tiles plc
The Gladstone Pottery Museum
Heritage Tile Conservation
Jackfield Tile Museum
Leeds City Museums
Liverpool Museum
The Minton Museum
The Museums & Galleries Commission
People's Palace Museum, Glasgow
Stoke-on-Trent City Museum & Art Gallery
Tolson Memorial Museum, Huddersfield
Williamson Art Gallery, Birkenhead
Yorkshire & Humberside Museums Council
Yorkshire Museum

Josie Montgomery
CURATOR OF ART
SCARBOROUGH ART GALLERY

PREFACE – THE LORD WEDGWOOD

Life moves in cycles as surely as the potter's wheel, but it is the lasting legacy of the past that affords us, and the following generations, the inspiration to develop our own style in the future.

This exhibition therefore not only illustrates our fascination with the past – the legacy of decorative tiles – but also underlines the work of today's craftsmen and women. Thus, as it travels the country, I am confident it will promote an increased interest and awareness in the contemporary tile market through its cultural roots.

As my own involvement in the tile market, via the comparatively recent formation of Fired Earth Tiles plc, comes in the 13th generation of a family tradition which spans over 200 years of ceramics, I think I might also claim that an old potter never dies – but sometimes he needs a new wheel!

Finally, I am particularly pleased to say that this comprehensive exhibition and catalogue represent a unique co-operation between the private sector (Fired Earth Tiles plc and Richard Dennis Publications), the public sector (Scarborough Art Gallery and the Museums & Galleries Commission) and the voluntary sector (Tiles & Architectural Ceramics Society). We are also indebted to the very many individual collectors and museums who have generously lent tiles for this unprecedented display – which is not just of benefit to us, but to all of those who will next carry 'the torch'. ❧

THE LORD WEDGWOOD
SEPTEMBER 1991

"...more architects are showing an interest in the innovative use of tiles..."

INTRODUCTION

Tiles have been a prominent part of Europe's cultural heritage since the Middle Ages. The word 'tile' comes from the Latin *tegula* and is formed from the verb *tegere* which means 'to cover'. Tiles have certainly been used to cover many surfaces, ranging from church and cathedral floors, cellars in Dutch houses, whole façades of buildings, porches, fireplaces, to bathrooms and even items of furniture. Their applications have been combined with an equally extensive range of different figurative designs and patterns, applied to the tile with the aid of diverse ceramic decoration techniques.

Tiles in the medieval period were produced in France, Germany and Britain between the 13th and 16th centuries. The most distinctive technique employed at that time was the 'inlaid' tile which consisted of imprinting a figure or pattern of white clay into the red body of the tile, which was then covered with a transparent lead glaze. Monastic churches, cathedrals and palaces often had magnificent floors made of inlaid tiles.

The Moorish occupation of Spain had transmitted the technique of tin-glazed pottery and tiles from the Middle East to Southern Europe. The technique consisted of painting in bright colours on a pure white ground. It spread from Spain and Italy to Northern Europe at the end of the 15th and beginning of the 16th centuries and this gave rise to the birth of the so-called 'delftware' industry in Holland and Britain. If tiles had been used on the floor in the Middle Ages, they now began to be used on the exterior and interior walls of buildings. The exterior use of tin-glazed tiles was very noticeable in Southern Europe where Portugal, in particular, developed a strong tradition for this kind of application. The Dutch found many interior uses for their tiles as can be seen in 17th and 18th century cellars, fireplaces

Hans van Lemmen DIP ART ATC BA
SENIOR LECTURER IN ART AND
DESIGN HISTORY
LEEDS POLYTECHNIC

9

Aerographed tile with printed 'WS' monogram on reverse (George Woolliscroft & Son, Hanley, Stoke-on-Trent); printed registration number 86882 (1887) and printed design number 402. (Private collection.)

and living rooms. Delftware tiles in Britain were mainly confined to the open fireplace. In Germany, Austria and Switzerland there developed a tradition for using painted and/or moulded tin-glazed plaques (*Kacheln*) for the decoration and construction of large free-standing stoves.

Until the middle of the 18th century tiles had been decorated by hand, but it was in Britain that the first experiments with printed decorations were conducted by John Sadler in Liverpool from 1756 onwards. Britain led the way in transforming an industry which was based on handwork and inherited craft skills into one based on machine production and mechanical decoration processes. The Industrial Revolution and tile-making are well illustrated by the example of Herbert Minton, who bought Prosser's patent for the pressing of tiles from powdered clay in 1840, opening the door to mass-production which led to the Victorian tile boom of the second half of the 19th century.

Britain was a major producer of tiles from the mid-19th to the beginning of the 20th centuries. Many now well-known china manufacturers made tiles, such as Minton, Wedgwood and Doulton. They were augmented by more specialist tile producers such as Maw & Co, Craven Dunnill and Godwin. New decoration techniques were developed and many designs were executed by now well-known Victorian architects, such as A W N Pugin, and artists such as Walter Crane. There also arose a backlash to the Industrial Revolution in the form of the Arts and Crafts Movement. Followers of this movement were involved in the production of hand-made and hand-decorated tiles, as the tiles of William Morris and William De Morgan amply demonstrated.

The heyday of decorative tiles had largely run its course by World War I. However, the Modernist reaction against excessive decoration meant more production of plain tiles. The Art Deco tiles of the 1920s and '30s reflected the interest in geometric abstract forms and stylized figurative subjects.

The 1960s and early '70s may come to be seen as a bleak spot in architectural history on two counts; the destruction of many fine tiled buildings and the clinical use of plain tiles in new ones. Conservation of the Victorian and Edwardian heritage during the '70s and '80s has revitalized the interest in decorative tiles. More and more architects are showing an interest in the innovative use of tiles in both the world of conservation as well as in new buildings. All this accompanies a more academic interest which has resulted in many publications providing us with a written and visual history of tiles. It all adds up to a healthy future for this particular branch of the decorative arts. ❧

"...designs on the tiles were of extreme delicacy..."

ISLAMIC TILES

The word 'Islamic' is used loosely to mean the tiles of the Near East, even though their origin goes back long before the dawn of the Islamic era (AD 622). Rudimentary tiles using a turquoise glaze have been found in Egypt, dating to the fourth millennium BC. The Assyrians and Babylonians from the 13th to 6th centuries BC made patterned wall tiles and the palace of the Achemenid kings at Susa, Persia (*c.*350 BC) had friezes of coloured relief tiles depicting lions, winged bulls and a frieze of archers of the royal bodyguard. Tile-making appears to have died out after the 4th century BC and neither the Greeks nor the Romans used glazed tiles. It was not until the Sassanian kings (AD 221–641) that glazed tile-making was revived, often combined with carved relief stucco using figures and plant forms.

After AD 641 the Islamic Empire spread rapidly and by the mid-8th century it occupied an area greater than the Roman Empire – from northern Spain to the borders of China. It was a period of conquest and reconquest with craftsmen following the conqueror either voluntarily or, more usually, by force. Consequently, there was a constant to-ing and fro-ing of styles and techniques.

The mosque of Sidi Oqba, at Kairouan (Tunisia), has tiles of the 9th century painted in opaque yellow and brown, showing traces of lustre. These were probably made by local potters who had migrated from Fatimid Egypt. When Saladin destroyed Fatimid buildings (in 1175) the potters moved from Egypt to Persia, settling at Raqqa (on the northern frontier of Syria and Mesopotamia) and Rayy (near Teheran, Iran). From 1200–1350 there was a flowering of tile production at Kashan (*kashani* is still used to mean 'tile' in modern Iran). The designs on the tiles were of extreme

Jon Catleugh
ARCHITECT
TRUSTEE OF THE DE MORGAN
FOUNDATION

11

delicacy, predominantly turquoise or yellow-gold lustre, sometimes in low-relief, often using star-shaped tiles alternating with cruciform tiles. Subjects included figures and animals as well as flowers and plant forms. In mosques, Koranic texts were used decoratively on bold relief tiles using Kufic and Nashki scripts in brilliant deep blue and gold.

After Timur's (Tamerlane) conquests from 1369 onwards, Samarkand was rebuilt as a capital city. A spectacular building of this period is the Timur Mausoleum, Samarkand (1404). Tile mosaics were used during this time. It was a laborious process whereby the pattern shapes are individually cut out and reassembled into slabs. The technique was used in Persia from the 14th century right through to the 17th century. One advantage of the technique was the avoidance of glazes running from one area to another in the kiln. Another way of avoiding colours running was called *de cuerda seca* ('dry cord') and was used a great deal in Moorish Spain; a greasy cord was laid along the pattern dividing lines to provide a dam. The cord burnt away in the kiln.

The earliest underglaze tiles were blue and white and showed a knowledge of Chinese patterns and motifs; there had been considerable trade with the Far East and ceramics were prized all along the Silk Route. By the end of the 15th century, a polychrome palette had been perfected using black, ochre, green, blue, turquoise and a brownish red.

The high point of Islamic tile production was at Isnik (Nicaea, northern Anatolia) from the end of the 15th century to the end of the 16th century. After the fall of Constantinople in 1453, the Ottoman capital was moved from Edirne and an intensive period of building commenced with extensive architectural use of tiles which varied in size from 9–13in and were usually made into panels framed by border tiles. Patterns were based primarily on flowers (cherry, tulip, carnation, rose and hyacinth) and trees (cypress). Isnik patterns were always conceived architecturally unlike most European tiles, which are more often than not based on a repetition of quite small motifs. The designers in Ottoman Turkey were under the patronage of the sultan and since tile and textile patterns were closely related, documented examples in one or other technique can be cross-related with some accuracy for dating. ❧

Moulded tile from Kashan, Persia, with Islamic script. 13th/14th century. (Victoria and Albert Museum.)

Select Bibliography

Y Petsopoulos (Ed.) *Tulips, Arabesques and Turbans*, Alexandria Press, London 1982

MEDIEVAL PAVING TILES

As far as is at present known, ornamental glazed-brick tiles made their first appearance in England at some time in the late-10th century. No other tiles of such an early date have yet been recorded in Western Europe, a priority shared with Anglo-Saxon glazed hollow-ware.

    The tiles referred to, though a small group found in only half-a-dozen places to date, as far apart as Winchester and York, are all so similar in technique that it is supposed they may be the work of one very small company of perhaps no more than two or three workers. In their day these tiles would have been rare and expensive and their use confined to the richer Anglo-Saxon minsters. Primitive decoration consisting of raised lines, and hence prone to wear, had, however, some advantages. The moulds could easily be made by carving grooves in the surface of a wooden board with a U-gouge and the raised fillets enabled glazes of different colours in the green-brown range to be used on the same tile. It is likely that the clay was *pushed* into the design rather than the pattern being *imprinted* by an intaglio stamp. Sizes ranged from 2.5in to 7.5in square.

    Some tiles of this group, from York, show zoomorphic subjects in high-relief and may indicate a rather later date for York work, foreshadowing tiles made during the great monastic revival of the 12th century. A floor of such tiles dating from 1161–66, excavated on the site of the Chapter House at St Albans Abbey, Hertfordshire, has decoration in high-relief detailed in sculptural style. Similar tiles, together with the kiln in which they were fired, were found at North Berwick, Lothian, (a Cistercian nunnery) and are now in the National Museum, Edinburgh. They have a Romanesque look and could date from before 1200. Of similar

Kenneth Beaulah FSA

Mosaic pavement of a type laid in Cistercian churches throughout Britain in the 13th century. 76in square, made in converse colours.

date to these high-relief tiles were others decorated in a diametrically opposite way – in other words line-ornament incised by hand. A tile of this sort was found embedded in a wall built between 1165 and 1167 at Orford Castle, Suffolk – a firm date.

The use of mosaic tiling on the Continent would have been well-known to English monks and masons by 1200 and plans, either from the beginning or for enlarging, being considered then or in the next half century would have been likely to have included mosaic floors of glazed-brick. Masonry rebated for tiles can be seen at several abbey sites in the north of Britain. The Cistercians in the region particularly favoured mosaic, perhaps because its abstract patterns were in line with the austere ideas governing decoration which were part of that order's precepts. The beginning of this fashion can be traced to the marble floors of Italy, such as may be seen in the Baptistery at Florence. A wish by northern churchmen to emulate these had its first expression probably in Germany, as the northern end of the Holy Roman Empire. Marble, however, being scarce, meant that paviours soon turned to brick which was so much easier to cut into shapes in its unfired state. France, too, adopted it but early on added ornament by 'inlaying'. German builders continued to use plain mosaic and it was probably the German form which arrived in England soon after 1200.

Mosaic relies for its effect on colour contrasts of adjacent pieces, achieved by coating the slabs of clay from which the light-coloured pieces were to be cut with a thin layer of white-burning clay. Half the number of such rolled-out slabs were left uncoated. Shapes were cut out by means of templates then, after firing, tiles from light and dark slabs were interchanged. The tilers travelled from one patron to another, taking their templates with them. Some of their contracts were enormous: the abbey churches at Byland, Fountains and Rievaulx (all Yorkshire) being 330, 370 and 375 feet long respectively, and the glazed tile paving extended into all corners of the buildings. Such great undertakings probably would not have been contemplated without the manual help of the lay brothers who were peculiar to the Cistercian order.

From the beginning the tilers in England improved and elaborated on their continental prototypes and by the time they arrived at Meaux Abbey (Humberside, previously Yorkshire) c.1250, their repertoire of designs had reached its greatest variety. To date, 269 designs are known with a probability of many more, since of one design in the form of a great wheel-window set in a square of 16 feet, only a few tiles have been found. The tilers at Meaux seem to have moved on before the floor of the church was finished as many of the loose tiles and fragments are of inferior work,

Mosaic tile made in nine sections forming the shape of a four-petalled flower. Meaux Abbey, c.1250. (Private collection.)

presumably from the hands of lay brothers. Among other degraded details these tiles have the white coating (engobe) brushed on instead of trowelled.

The practice of coating with engobe proved to be an important step forward, as from it probably developed the two-colour inlaid tile. The Yorkshire mosaic workers occasionally added an 'inlaid' ornament or else the impression of a stamp on an engobe-coated tile, without infilling. When such a tile wore down to the clay body it looked like an intended two-colour tile and must at once have suggested a means of manufacture, i.e. by pressing a stamp deeply into the white engobe then removing engobe until the white was left only in the pattern. It is generally possible to find on a medieval two-colour tile an imprint of the stamp on top of the engobe. Sometimes it is the merest trace, but it could not have got there except in the way described above.

So-called 'printed' tiles are the same, only with a very thin coating of engobe. Enlarging on this technicality, there is a 13th century tile from Rievaulx, in the British Museum, which has four round depressions clearly visible on the engobe of an 'inlaid' tile. These must have been made by the heads of nails used to hold down a fretted metal plate which had been made to repair or replace a broken wooden stamp. The tile is illustrated as design 2,670 in the two-volume British Museum *Catalogue*. No explanation is advanced there to account for the marks. Part of the design on the same tile is a chalice with the foot missing – a detail no doubt thought too small to repair by the same means. The nail-heads and other features, such as differences between two tiles from the same stamp and a kind of 'edging' to the designs, all result directly from the 'stamp-on-engobe' method. It should be said here, however, that a method of making moulded cavities on the clay body, then filling with engobe, was sometimes employed. A prime example is the fine series of tiles from Chertsey Abbey, Surrey. The precise outlines seen on these tiles could not have been achieved by other means.

Contemporary with the plain-tile mosaics but having a later start in this country were the decorated mosaics of French antecedents such as those made in 1244–5 for a chapel on an upper floor in Henry III's palace at Clarendon, Wiltshire. Part of a large circle and reconstruction of part of the kiln from Clarendon form a prominent exhibit in the Medieval Tile Room at the British Museum. Related to the Clarendon tiles, but somewhat later and more refined, is the extraordinary pavement formerly at Jervaulx Abbey, North Yorkshire and another now at Kirkstall Abbey, Leeds.

The church floor at Jervaulx, when first uncovered, showed large parts of eight 7ft-diameter circles and indications where another four had been. Most of the rest of the floor was occupied by squares of 36 decorated

Inlaid tile with knight on horseback. Dunstable Priory, 13th century. (Private collection.)

tiles set within a criss-cross of plain black ones. By a great misfortune the pavement was left exposed through a winter soon after the floor had been cleared of rubble in 1807. Frost reduced it largely to chips. On the Jervaulx tiles the surface where it was not covered by engobe had been darkened, thus enhancing the designs. This effect can be seen even on tiles with pale-coloured body clay. The effect, perhaps at first accidental, seems to have been produced intentionally, perhaps by management of the kiln atmosphere. Incidentally, these tiles do not show any imprints of stamps. Most of the Jervaulx–Kirkstall tiles were made in converse colours. This may have been made easier by the process used – whatever that was.

From about 1240, 'inlaid' quarries (quarry simply means 'square') gradually gained ground over mosaic, and because square tiles could be turned out so much more expeditiously than shaped pieces, they held the field after labour became scare in the wake of the Black Death (1347–50).

The last phase of mosaic work, in the early years of the 14th century, saw sgraffito and line-impressed decoration used extensively, the best known examples being in Prior Crauden's Chapel, Ely Cathedral, Cambridgeshire, c.1324. Adjacent pieces were no longer all in contrasting colours but large figures such as Adam and Eve (or it might be a lion) were made of tiles of one colour, the divisions cutting across forms, similar to the leading of a stained glass window. The term *opus sectile* has been given to this kind of work.

Thus it will be seen that between the introduction of 'inlaid' patterning, c.1240, and the middle of the 14th century, all the processes used throughout the medieval era had been discovered. By this time also, a great change had come over the organization of the tile industry.

We have seen that monasteries were the principal users in the early years. When foundations, watercourses and fishponds were being dug, ample supplies of clay would have been available at most sites. To sustain large tiling schemes (for work such as floors and roofs) kilns were generally built close to the building site, to be abandoned on the building's completion. The tilers then moved on.

From 1300 onwards, however, decorated tiles began to be bought for parish churches. The tiles were chiefly used in the eastern part of a church but the sheer number of customers, mainly in the southern counties, led to the emergence of a large industry operating from settled 'factories' where suitable clay and fuel were available. Their wares were transported to users mainly by water. South of a line between the rivers Humber and Ribble, 58 kilns, or evidence of them, have been found. North of that line, there were only six.

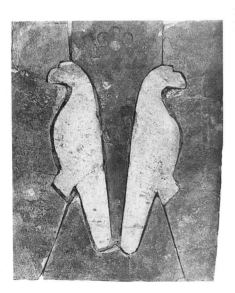

Mosaic tile made in six sections showing a pair of stylized doves. Meaux Abbey, c.1250. (Private collection.)

The rest of the story consists for the most part of cutting corners technically. When innovation dried up there was not much to choose between the tiles of one factory and another. Price seems to have been the chief deciding factor, and since the cost of transport was heavy the nearest kiln would be likely to get the order. Some really execrable tiles were delivered and even fixed in floors. This must have been a chief cause of the final disappearance of demand. The dissolution of the monasteries, which occurred about the same time (1537–39) need not necessarily have been a prime cause, others being the arrival of polychrome tiles from the Low Countries and from Spain, and the availability of well-made, large floor tiles from Flanders. A flash-in-the-pan came in the shape of a series of very fine tiles custom-made for Thornbury Castle, Gloucestershire, and Hailes Abbey, Gloucestershire, after 1500, but the force of changing fashion could not be resisted and English manufacture of decorated tiles was almost extinct by 1550.

As a postscript it can be related that at Meaux Abbey versions of the 13th century mosaics have been found, but of much inferior workmanship compared with earlier work. These badly-made tiles have recently been dated, by finds at Fountains Abbey, to the 15th century. This is of interest in showing that the original floor, then over 200 years old, was admired enough for reproductions to be ordered for repairs. ❧

Note: The word 'inlay' has been put in quotation marks because forcing engobe into the tile body is not truly inlaying. The word, however, does correctly apply to 19th century church floor tiles.

16-tile pattern from Hailes Abbey, Gloucestershire, made shortly before the dissolution as a memorial to Abbot Thomas Stafford (1483–1503). The letter 'T', his pastoral staff, and the letters 'FORD' make up his rebus.

Select Bibliography

E S Eames *Catalogue of Medieval Lead-glaze Earthenware Tiles in the British Museum*, 2 Vols., British Museum Publications, London 1980
E S Eames *English Medieval Tiles*, British Museum Publications, London 1985
E C Norton *Cistercian Art and Architecture in the British Isles*, Cambridge University Press, Cambridge 1986

"...literally millions of tiles were produced..."

TIN-GLAZED TILES

Hans van Lemmen DIP ART ATC BA
SENIOR LECTURER IN ART AND
DESIGN HISTORY
LEEDS POLYTECHNIC

Early-17th century tin-glazed Dutch wall tile with a tulip, grapes, pomegranates and a quarter star in blue, orange, green and purple. The influence of the southern maiolica tradition is evident. (Private collection.)

The history of tin-glazed tiles in Europe goes back at least to the 14th century. The technique consisted of painting with ceramic pigments on unfired white tin-glaze, which sank into the glaze during the firing and fused permanently with it. This technique is known as 'in-glaze'. The tradition of tin-glazed ceramics was transmitted to Spain via the Middle East with the Muslim conquest of the Iberian Peninsula. The splendid 14th century tiles at the Alhambra, painted in blue and golden-yellow lustre on a white ground and bearing the Arabic motto, *'And there is no conqueror but God'*, may have been produced at Malaga or Granada. The use of cobalt blue as a ceramic pigment on tin-glaze with lustre, was first used in Europe in Spain. Spanish pottery of this period is now known as 'Hispano-Moresque'. Valencia became an important centre for painted tin-glazed tiles in the 15th century. The striking Valencian blue and golden-brown or yellow lustre combination, on a white ground, became the most sought after luxury pottery in late-medieval Europe.

Interesting documentary evidence has survived that records some of the early commissions for these products. From archival accounts we learn that the Dukes of Burgundy (Philip the Bold, John the Fearless and Philip the Good) and their relations, such as Duke Jean de Berry, were early patrons of tin-glazed tiles for their various residences throughout France at the end of the 14th and beginning of the 15th centuries. These rulers were given to pomp and display, and having floors paved with tin-glazed tiles showing their own coats-of-arms executed in blue and lustre would have added to their display of wealth and power. Such tiles were made by Spanish craftsmen on site. The lustre tile pavements for the Palais de

Justice, Poitiers, commissioned by Duke Jean de Berry, were made by Jehan de Valence (from Valencia, Spain), nicknamed 'le Sarrazin', in 1384. The accounts that have survived go into some detail about the materials used for the construction of the kilns and the materials needed for the production of the tiles. Very few tiles made for either Duke Jean de Berry or the Dukes of Burgundy have survived, but some idea of what they were like can be seen in the paintings of artists such as Jan van Eyck, who was in the employ of the Duke of Burgundy and must have seen similar tiles at his court. The very accurate way in which Van Eyck represented objects in his paintings may provide us with some visual information about late-14th and early-15th century tin-glazed tiles. His magnificent *Madonna with Canon Joris van der Paele* (1434) in Bruges, Belgium, with blue-and-white floor tiles showing Spanish interlacing motifs is a case in point.

Potters in France and the Low Countries in the 14th century occasionally produced small quantities of tin-glazed tiles alongside contemporary lead-glazed inlaid floor tiles. A few examples painted in green and purple have come to light, as at the Palace of the Popes, Avignon; the church of St Julien, Brioude; and at the Abbaye des Dunes, Koksijde, on the Belgian coast. These seem to have been isolated incidents, and it was not until the beginning of the 16th century that regular production centres of tin-glazed tile manufacture began to develop in Northern Europe under the influence of Italian pottery.

The technique of tin-glazed pottery spread to Italy from Spain. Italian tin-glazed pottery and tiles are known as 'maiolica'. In Italy, tiles were used on the floor. Characteristic is the combination of square and hexagonal tiles painted with floral, heraldic and animal subjects as well as many fine portraits. Important centres of production were Faenza, Siena, Deruta and Florence. A distinctive maiolica palette developed, consisting of blue, orange, green, yellow and purple. The tile pavement in the Vaselli Chapel, Church of San Petronio, Bologna, dated 1487, depicting a large range of finely painted decorative patterns and figurative motifs, shows Italian maiolica tile manufacture at its best. From Italy, the tradition of tin-glazed floor tiles spread north at the beginning of the 16th century. Italian potters were active at Lyon, France, from 1512 onwards. Elsewhere in France, they settled at Nevers, and at Rouen we find the workshop of Masseot Abaquesne, who carried out important floor and wall tile schemes for the Château d'Ecouen, around 1542.

The activities of Guido di Savino, who emigrated from Castel Durante, Italy, to Antwerp, Flanders, at the beginning of the 16th century, are well recorded. In Antwerp he set up a thriving family business and after

Hexagonal tin-glazed floor tiles with the portrait of a man in dark blue, yellow and green. Probably made c.1520 in the workshop of Guido Andries in Antwerp. These tiles are in the Vyne Chapel, Sherborne St John, near Basingstoke, Hampshire.

marrying a local woman changed his name to Guido Andries. It may well be that the maiolica tiles at the Vyne Chapel, near Basingstoke, Hampshire, are from his workshop. The political troubles that engulfed Antwerp during the second half of the 16th century led to potters moving to Holland and England. Two potters who moved to England were Jasper Andries (son of Guido Andries) and Jacob Jansen. Both moved to Norwich in 1567. They went to London in 1570 where they petitioned Elizabeth I for the making of tin-glazed pottery and tiles. Other Flemish potters settled in Holland in such places as Middelburg and Haarlem, from where they passed on their skills to native potters, and here we can see the beginning of what would become known as the 'delftware industry' in both Holland and England.

If the tradition of Italian maiolica spread north during the 16th century, it must not be forgotten that during this period Portugal began to produce tin-glazed tiles called *azulejos*. Until then, the Portuguese had imported Spanish tiles, some of which can still be seen at the Royal Palace of Sintra. Tiles were also imported from Antwerp and Northern Italy during the middle of the 16th century. Under the influence of these imported products, Portuguese production of painted tin-glazed tiles began at Lisbon. The Portuguese tile industry grew enormously during the 17th and 18th centuries and nowhere else in Europe was the tile used so extensively as an architectural feature. Tiles were employed on a large scale in churches, monasteries and palaces, as can be seen in the chapel at Santo Amaro, Lisbon, and at the Palace of Fronteira, Bemfica (near Lisbon), where there are tile schemes dating from around 1670. The fashion for tiles filtered down to most forms of public and domestic architecture. One result is that Portuguese tiles are always designed for large wall areas and are meant to be seen as part of all-over decorative and figurative schemes. There are, therefore, less individual tile designs as is so common, for example, among Dutch and English delftware. The latter are so very collectable today because each tile is often an independent unit while a single Portuguese tile is less meaningful as it is usually only a fragment of a much larger design.

The term 'delftware' is derived from the Dutch town of Delft, where from the 17th century onwards many potteries produced hand-painted tin-glazed pottery of high quality which was exported all over the world. The potteries in Delft produced tiles alongside their other ware, but most Dutch tiles were made at places such as Rotterdam, Utrecht, Harlingen and Makkum. The Dutch developed a much larger range of subjects on individual tiles than can be found anywhere else in Europe during the 17th and 18th centuries. This has partly to do with the fact that Dutch houses were relatively small, where tiles would be used in cellars,

Mid-18th century English tin-glazed tile made in London. Painted in blue with a scene depicting the baptism of Christ. (Private collection.)

fireplaces and as wall skirtings. It would have been less appropriate, or even impossible, to have employed large all-over design schemes, but there was also the rich and diverse Dutch pictorial tradition in paintings and prints that played a role. Dutch 17th century paintings and prints showed great specialization in different kinds of subject matter. Prints often served as models for tile designs. Taking the 17th century in isolation we find themes and subjects such as flowers, birds, animals, portraits, soldiers, horsemen, trades and occupations, biblical subjects, children's games, ships, shepherds and shepherdesses, and many different kinds of landscape. In the case of figurative tiles they usually featured corner motifs which became independent decorative motifs when four tiles were placed together. In this way larger schemes could be created with great effect. Tile panels were also produced but they were often special commissions for large houses.

Dutch tin-glazed tiles were exported in large numbers, particularly to France, Germany and Britain, where delftware pottery and tiles were much prized by royalty and the aristocracy. William III, for example, had Dutch tiles (designed by Daniele Morot) installed in the dairy at Hampton Court, while under the reign of Louis XIV thousands of Dutch tiles were used to line the bathroom at Château de Marly, Marly-le-Roi, Louveciennes, in 1688. The Dutch could export on such a large scale because they had specialist tile factories in operation where literally millions of tiles were produced. The Rotterdam tile factories were particularly prolific in their output. In neighbouring countries tiles were usually a sideline of potteries making tin-glazed pottery and, therefore, the output of tiles was much smaller.

Although tin-glazed pottery in Britain go back to the latter half of the 16th century, the 'delftware' industry only became significant during the 18th century when tiles and pottery were produced in considerable quantities in London, Bristol, Liverpool and Glasgow. English and Scottish delftware tiles show their dependence on the Dutch products, but specific British features did develop, particularly in the form of corner motifs and borders, *bianco-sopra-bianco* decoration, and polychromatic designs. Despite native production, and at times import embargoes, Dutch tiles continued being imported in great numbers, as can still be seen in many houses throughout the British Isles.

In Germany, Austria and Switzerland, tin-glazed tiles were made in connection with the large stoves which were traditional forms of heating in Central Europe from the late-15th century onwards. In many respects the tile history of these German-speaking countries is dominated by the

Mid-19th century French tin-glazed tile depicting a cock within a circular frame painted in blue. Probably made at either Ponchon or St Paul near Beauvais (Oise). (Private collection.)

production of stove tiles. They even have two separate words for tiles. *Fliesen* are wall or floor tiles; but *Kacheln* are stove tiles (the word *Kachel* in German means 'stove'). Stove tiles were made in relief to create a larger surface for the radiation of heat. In Germany during the 18th century there were also several potteries manufacturing tin-glazed tiles in imitation of Dutch tiles. They often operated with the help of Dutch potters. Production could not keep pace with demand and large quantities of Dutch tiles were imported, as can still be seen at the Amalienburg Hunting Lodge, Nymphenburg; in the very large tiled cellars at Caputh Castle, near Potsdam, and at Oranienbaum Castle, near Dessau. There were tin-glaze potteries in Berlin, Dresden and Neurenberg, but one factory that made more original German tiles was at Ansbach. Here, in 1765, some 2,800 tiles were made for the Residenz Palace in Ansbach showing flowers, birds, hunting, oriental and pastoral scenes painted with great delicacy and executed in polychrome.

In Northern Europe changes in pottery production techniques during the second half of the 18th century and the advent of wallpaper were responsible for a steep decline in the manufacture of delftware. This process accelerated during the 19th century when machine production techniques began to replace hand-made tile manufacture. A limited production was still carried on in France at Desvres, Pas-de-Calais, and around Beauvais, Oise, while in Holland such firms as Ravesteijn in Utrecht and Tjallingi and Van Hulst in Harlingen maintained production. The 20th century saw a further decline in output. Since 1980, however, a growing interest in hand-made tiles has meant a boost for the tin-glazed variety. Several firms such as Tichelaar in Makkum, Holland, are still producing hand-painted tiles based on traditional motifs, thus maintaining direct links with the great tradition of tin-glazed tile production of the 17th and 18th centuries. ❧

Dutch tile-painter at work today. The scene is painted on the unfired white tin-glaze which requires great sureness of touch. After painting the tile is fired.

Select Bibliography

H van Lemmen *Delftware Tiles*, Shire Publications, Princes Risborough, 1986
C Norton 'Medieval Tin-glazed Painted Tiles in North-West Europe' in *Medieval Archaeology*, Vol XXVIII, 1984

"...Wright's patent had been the foundation of a great industry..."

ENCAUSTIC FLOOR TILES

By 1830 the neo-Gothic style of architecture was well launched. Parker's *Glossary of Architecture*, 1836, almost ignored the existence of the Classical school and went a long way, by selected dated examples, to provide the study of Gothic architecture with a factual base. The third edition, 1840, had two coloured plates of 40 medieval tiles (for the first time in print, accurately drawn) and in the following year John Gough Nichols had published the first section of a work in four parts presenting good illustrations of a further 100 examples. All this came too late to help form the policy of Samuel Wright, the pioneer in the manufacture of decorated pavement tiles who in the 1820s had already completed experiments and by 1830 had received the grant of a patent for his process. Unfortunately, his tiles, white-bodied with Moorish-inspired decoration in black, appealed neither to house nor to church builders and after five years, during which his sales did not reach a profitable level, he sold his equipment and a large amount of remaining stock to Herbert Minton.

Minton was head of the china-making company situated not far from Wright's works in Stoke-on-Trent, Staffordshire, and it would have been well known to Wright that Minton had had a similar ambition, and from possibly an earlier date. Through Minton's acquaintance with A W N Pugin, which later developed into a warm friendship, he received good advice about the sort of tiles that church architects wanted.

Wright's work proved to be of little use to Minton, who wanted his designs to be in yellow or buff on a brown background, in the medieval style. The alteration of Wright's formula for inlay clay from black to white caused Minton much trouble through its shrinking more than the body of

Kenneth Beaulah FSA

Chamberlain glazed encaustic floor tile of the early 1840s. (Private collection.)

the tiles and coming loose. The 19th century ceramic historian, Llewellynn Jewitt, tells how the foundations of roads surrounding the Minton works at Stoke-on-Trent were made up of cart-loads of spoiled tiles. It took Minton five years (to 1840) before he had overcome this and other difficulties. The only tiles made by Wright (at present known) were supplied by Minton c.1837, out of old stock, to pave the entrance hall of Sir J P Orde's mansion, Kilmory Castle, near Lochgilphead, Argyll (now the Council Offices of Argyll and Bute). The floor is still in very good condition.

Part of Wright's bargain with Minton was that he should retain the patent rights and receive a ten per cent royalty. To guard against a patentee losing interest Wright made a similar arrangement with Walter Chamberlain (subsequently taken over by two other partners) of the Worcester Porcelain Co, who was looking for something to keep his men in work after completion of *a huge table service for Royalty*. Chamberlain was friendly with Harvey Eginton, County Surveyor of Worcestershire, an antiquary who in 1833 had discovered a medieval tile kiln at Malvern. So both licensees (Minton and Chamberlain) had the benefit of design assistance from architects working in the neo-Gothic style. Minton was a perfectionist who could not satisfy himself with the quality of his product, while Chamberlain was content with a rougher finish and consequently was supplying tiles for a year or more before Minton was ready. Yet it was Minton who secured the first big tiling contract which attracted publicity enough to establish his firm as a front-runner. For that job (Temple Church, off Strand, London) he devised a way of enhancing the patterns by painting over the inlay clay (engobe) with an opaque yellow glaze or enamel, the body of the tile remaining unglazed. This was a process used by Minton and no other firm until 1866 at the earliest.

A document in the Minton archive hints at the existence of other licensees, but the two named, for practical purposes, had the field to themselves until 1851 when the patent and a seven-year extension which they had jointly bought from Wright finally expired.

Chamberlain's tiles did not depart from the yellow-and-brown medieval style, while Minton, as early as 1843, had adopted for his more expensive tiles blue-and-white engobe which promoted their popularity.

Preparing for the expiry of the patent, other makers had been getting ready for entry into this lucrative trade. Maw & Co stepped in in 1850 by buying out Chamberlain's (Worcester) tile department. In 1852 this firm moved from Worcester to Broseley, Shropshire, and in 1883 to nearby Jackfield (in the Ironbridge Gorge). Within a few years Maw & Co spanned the world with their decorated pavements.

Minton unglazed encaustic floor tile for a church depicting the stigmata of Christ, c.1860. (Private collection.)

In 1852 Henry Godwin, who had worked at Maw & Co's Worcester factory, left that firm to help his brother, William, turn the latter's brickyard into a prosperous tile-making concern at Lugwardine, near Hereford. In 1854 F G Sanders opened the Architectural Pottery Co, Poole, Dorset, mainly for exploiting a patent for producing 'tessellated' tiles. However, finding the process unprofitable, he soon turned to making inlaid tiles by Minton's well-tried method. The technical man in the partnership was John Ridgway, the well-known china maker, of Stoke-on-Trent.

If we may extrapolate the condition of the trade in one area – the old East Riding of Yorkshire – to the United Kingdom as a whole, we can say that sales had reached their highest pitch by 1875, and that Samuel Wright's patent had been the foundation of a great industry employing thousands of workers.

So far, we have only been dealing with church tiles, but there was another very important branch of paving-tile manufacture which relied on the same process for its decorative component. Minton once again was the trail-blazer. The body of these new tiles was 'cane-coloured', to use Minton's own term. The body was not intended to be glazed, and was almost invariably inlaid with engobes of two, or usually more colours. The body clay was very hard and being unglazed was not slippery. The tiles were specially recommended for public buildings or corridors of large houses. St George's Hall, Liverpool (1852) and Leeds Town Hall (1858) are outstanding examples of public buildings which used Minton's new tiles. The Classical style in architecture was often still favoured for those purposes and patterns on the tiles were designed to match. Instead of fleurs-de-lis, quatrefoils and rouleaux we see the acanthus, anthemion (flower-like ornament) and guilloche (ornament imitating braided ribbons). They were introduced about 1850 but their time-span did not extend for more than about 20 years. The Classical mode became more tenuous, giving way before Gothic, until demand was so small that manufacture was abandoned. 'Civic tiles' is a useful term for describing this genre.

In view of the fact that these heavy tiles, one-inch thick for the most part, were purely commercial productions, it is noteworthy that their makers went to some trouble to mark them on the back in a way which presents much information. There was the maker's name impressed in large letters, and, in the case of Minton, the 'clock-number' of the workman for piece-work and inspection purposes. Craven Dunnill stamped their tiles with the mould number and a prefix indicating which engobe to use. One often finds a diamond-shaped mark showing that the design was a registered one. This mark was allocated officially by the Designs Registry

Godwin glazed encaustic floor tile for a church depicting a fish, c.1865. (Private collection.)

25

and gives the date when registered and how to trace the filed copy. Minton often imprinted their year mark – a symbol indicating when the tile had been made, and this is sometimes accompanied by a letter standing for the month. These marks, either together or separately, were pressed into the clay in its soft state.

The method of manufacture has often been described and is simple enough in theory. The design was carved into the face of a flat block of plaster, the carving taking the form of flat-bottomed channels with sloping sides about 2mm deep. A cast was taken from this in plaster, now in relief, and this was used as the working mould. The hand-carved original was kept safe for further casts as and when moulds became worn or damaged. A cast-iron frame equal in depth to the tile's thickness was placed over the relief mould which was then filled with plastic clay and consolidated in a hand press. On withdrawing from the press the back markings were pressed into the clay. The frame was turned over and the cavities formed by the mould were filled with clay of contrasting colour and with a consistency similar to soft butter. While still in its frame the surplus engobe was scraped away leaving the design clean and sharp-edged. The tile in its frame was laid aside for a few days. When it had shrunk enough for easy separation from the frame the sides were shaved with a kind of potato-peeler and the tile was left for some weeks until dry enough for the kiln. Glazing needed a second firing.

This process bore little resemblance to the medieval one. The finished tiles, too, cannot be confused. Whereas the Victorian tile depended on a stamp precisely outlined, the medieval process showed much variety of outline caused by a varying thickness of surface engobe through which a stamp had to be pressed.

Antiquarians deprecated the mechanical look of tiles formed by Wright's patent, but everyone else liked them claiming, logically, that medieval tilers would have equalled that accuracy if they could. Manufacture of inlaid ('encaustic') tiles was largely confined to an area bounded, clockwise, by Stoke-on-Trent, Coalville (Leicestershire), Worcester, Hereford, Jackfield and Ruabon, North Wales.

The method so far described was known as the 'plastic clay' process. Greatly increased productivity became possible after 1840 by the use of powdered clay under Prosser's patent, though decorated 'inlaid' tiles could not be made of powder-clay until Boulton and Worthington's patent of 1854. Thin metal masks or stencils, of the thickness of what was to be the engobe, were laid successively in the bottom of the mould-frame and variously coloured powdered clays were introduced before the frame was filled up with powdered body-clay and consolidated under heavy pressure. It need hardly be said that this description is a great simplification. Powder-clay tiles can be recognized by the maker's name and back markings being in relief through the use of an intaglio-engraved back plate. Plastic clay continued to be used by some makers as an alternative right up to the time when production finally ceased early in the 20th century.

Despite the fact that inlaid tiles were the only kind of decorated flooring which would withstand a lot of wear (apart from mosaic) the hand processes which were economically possible in the 19th century became too expensive in the 20th. This, and the swing from fashion, brought about their termination.

There is a strange twist in this story: inlaid tiles were being made in Flanders from the Middle Ages until about 1920 by the medieval process described previously. If Minton had known about these tiles he could perhaps have saved himself a great deal of trouble and expense. In *The Art Journal*, 1849, there was a description of them: '...*if we break an ornamented Dutch tile it is evident that the upper surface is impressed by a stamp. The ornaments are* en creux. *The cavities are filled with a finer paste. Considerable skill is required to ensure the equal contraction of the fine and coarse clay*'. ('Dutch Tiles' at this date was the trade name for imported brown-and-yellow tiles of medieval type. Blue-and-white tin-glazed tiles from Holland were known as 'Delft Tiles'.) ⁊

Select Bibliography

J Barnard *Victorian Ceramic Tiles*, Studio Vista/Christie's, London 1972
K Beaulah *Church Tiles*, Shire Publications, Princes Risborough 1987
W J Furnival *Leadless Decorative Tiles, Faience and Mosaic*, Furnival (privately
    published), Stone 1904

"...both Minton firms showed the whole spectrum of 19th century design styles..."

MINTON TILES

Hans van Lemmen DIP ART ATC BA
SENIOR LECTURER IN ART AND
DESIGN HISTORY
LEEDS POLYTECHNIC

Herbert Minton (1793–1858), regarded by many as the father of the 19th century British tile industry.

The name 'Minton' carries a certain amount of reverence in the tile world – and for good reason. The firm of Minton had, throughout the 19th century, been at the forefront of technological and artistic innovation with remarkable results. As early as 1835, Herbert Minton had taken a share in Samuel Wright's patent for making encaustic tiles which became a great success story for him, particularly after paving the floor of Temple Church, London, in 1842. Business was helped along further with the aid of royal patronage and the fruitful association with Augustus Welby Pugin who not only used Minton's products but also designed encaustic tiles for him.

In 1840 Minton realized the significance and potential of Prosser's invention of pressing dust-clay in a machine and took a share in the patent and adapted it to pressing tiles. Wall tiles could then be mass-produced and decorated with transfer prints or other suitable methods. By 1842 Minton had over 60 tile presses in operation. Prince Albert took an interest in Minton's endeavours and was present at a soirée in March 1843 when the method of pressing dust-clay was shown to a distinguished assembly. Royal commissions included supplying encaustic tiles for Osborne House, Isle of Wight (1845–49), and the tiles for the Royal Dairy, Frogmore, Windsor, in 1858. Of great importance was the commission to tile the floors and fireplaces of the Palace of Westminster according to Pugin's designs. The firm also showed many of their tiles at the Great Exhibition, 1851, of which Pugin's large stove for the Medieval Court was one of the great show-pieces of Minton's majolica tile production.

After Herbert Minton's death in 1858 the firm carried on in the form of two departments. One concentrated on tiles, under the direction of

Michael Daintry Hollins, while the china department was managed by Colin Minton Campbell. This partnership ended in 1868 when both departments became independent firms. Hollins continued the tile business under the name of Minton, Hollins & Co, while Campbell carried on under the name Minton's China Works. The break-up of the Minton firm was not without rancour. Both firms produced a large range of tiles and rivalry between them was strong. Encaustic floor tiles were the exclusive province of Minton, Hollins & Co and they kept on using the treasured back-stamp of Minton & Co which had been in use since the early 1840s. On the front of many of their catalogues one finds, *'The Patents for the manufacture of Encaustic and Plain Tiles belonged exclusively to, and were carried out by this Firm, who have the sole right to the use of the name 'Minton' and 'Patent' in the manufacture and sale of these Tiles. All Tiles made by this Firm bear the impression 'Minton & Co' or 'Minton, Hollins & Co'.'* They also manufactured many picture-tile series, some of which were designed by John Moyr Smith and W P Simpson.

Minton's China Works produced wall tiles only and was able to attract a considerable number of first-rate artists who also designed for tiles. Unlike their rivals Minton, Hollins & Co, they did not stress possession of technical patents and the name 'Minton', but rather went for artistic pedigree. They claimed credit for the employment of the famous A W N Pugin as a tile designer in their catalogues and prefaced many of them with the words, *'The process for the decoration of tiles was early favoured by the late Mr A Welby Pugin, 'the great restorer of Gothic Art', in the Houses of Parliament and in many other places, and the patterns of that style of ornament in this book are all from his hand.'*

There is no doubt that Minton's China Works managed to enlist the services of more prominent designers than Minton, Hollins & Co. Louis Marc Solon, John Moyr Smith, Christopher Dresser, Stacy Marks, William Wise, Antonin Boullemier and L T Swetnam were some whose work can be seen on their tiles. The list of eminent designers makes it clear that Minton's China Works retained the artistic leadership of the Minton firms after the break-up of 1868. John Moyr Smith in particular designed many well-known picture-tile series of which the *Waverley Novels*, *Old Testament*, *New Testament*, *Early English History*, *Idylls of the King*, *Fables* and the *Shakespeare* series are some of the better known ones. Minton's China Works tile catalogues of the 1880s and '90s show the wide range of pictorial and patterned designs they produced. Campbell was also instrumental in setting up Minton's Art Pottery Studio in Kensington Gore, London, in 1871, where high quality painted tiles were produced until the studio burned down in 1875.

Minton unglazed encaustic floor tile for a church depicting the Holy Lamb, c.1860. (Private collection.)

Both Minton firms showed the whole spectrum of 19th century design styles: Gothic and romantic medievalism, Renaissance and rococo, the influences of China and Japan, Persian and Arts and Crafts, as well as Art Nouveau. Technically the tiles showed many different decoration techniques such as transfer printing, machine relief moulding, slip trailing, hand painting and *pâte-sur-pâte*. Their output was quite enormous and millions of tiles were produced for a great variety of different purposes.

The fortunes of the Minton firms in the 20th century were very mixed. Minton's China Works curtailed tile production in the years leading up to World War I, and it was not resumed afterwards. Minton, Hollins & Co kept up production, but had to adapt to a changed economic climate and different design fashions. The fashion for tiles became more utilitarian and they were often plain, mottled or coated with eggshell glazes as can be seen in bathrooms and fireplaces of the inter-war period, but decorative tiles were not entirely squeezed out. The firm survived the economic difficulties of World War II, and continued tile manufacture until the early 1960s when they merged with H & R Johnson-Richards Tiles Ltd. ❧

Back-mark used on Minton's China Works tiles (c. 1868–1900) showing the firm's globe trade mark.

Select Bibliography

E Aslin & P Atterbury *Minton 1798–1910*, Victoria and Albert Museum & Thomas Goode & Co Ltd, London 1976

P Atterbury & M Batkin *The Dictionary of Minton*, Antique Collectors' Club, Woodbridge 1990

V Cecil *Minton Majolica*, Jeremy Cooper Ltd, London 1982

D S Skinner & H van Lemmen *Minton Tiles 1835–1935*, Stoke-on-Trent City Museum & Art Gallery, Stoke-on-Trent 1984

> *"...the largest decorative tile works in the world..."*

MAW TILES

The development of Maw & Co as one of the leading tile manufacturers in Britain in the 19th century was closely dependent on the Maw family. As 'art manufacturers' their tile-making efforts progressed from a hand-pressed prototype in the 1840s to the creation in Jackfield, Shropshire, of the largest decorative tile works in the world, little more than 30 years later.

The key characters were the brothers George and Arthur Maw and their father, John Hornby Maw. The family had come from a farming background in Lincolnshire but the essential financial backing for developing the tile works must have been made possible by J H Maw's involvement in his successful manufacturing chemist's business in London. In 1839 he withdrew from this business and pursued his artistic talents with a circle of friends whilst living in Hastings, Sussex. The circle included J M W Turner, J S Cotman and David Cox. Against such a strongly artistic and cultural home background it is not difficult to imagine the young George and Arthur Maw acquiring skills and attitudes which were to re-emerge in the tile business.

The Maws' tile-making venture appears to have started almost by chance. A family journal records that they moved from Hastings to Tavistock, Devon, in 1849, John Hornby Maw *'having heard of certain beds of porcelain clay for sale on Dartmoor which he thought might prove a good investment for his sons'*. Nothing came of this and after four months the family moved on to Bideford, North Devon. Here, father and sons were inspired to attempt the reproduction of a medieval encaustic tile after observing the simple techniques of one of the local potters. George and Arthur's sister, Anne Mary, recorded in her journal that, *'my mother and I*

Tony Herbert BSC DIP CONS
ADVISER ON HISTORIC TILES AND
ARCHITECTURAL CERAMICS

Maw transfer-printed and hand-painted nursery tile designed by Walter Crane, 1864. (Private collection.)

made pilgrimages to old village churches in the neighbourhood where I, prone upon my knees, industriously traced the designs of all the ancient encaustic pavements we could find'.

In the autumn of 1849 J H Maw's attention was drawn to an advertisement for the sale of an 'Encaustic Tile Works' in Worcester. In 1850 the Maws moved to Worcester and took over the remnants of Walter Chamberlain's works. They continued using old dies and their tiles were primarily buff- and red-patterned encaustics.

In the spring of 1852, attracted by the prospect of good, cheap, local clay and coal, the family and its workforce migrated to Broseley in the Ironbridge Gorge, Shropshire. The move must have been an extraordinary sight as the Maws, the tribe of workmen, their equipment, their wives, children and belongings all came in the same train! Maw & Co's first Benthall Works was on a cramped site bisected by a main road ('BENTHALL, BROSELEY' on back-marks).

Production of tiles grew steadily and in these early years Maw & Co advanced on two fronts. They consolidated and then expanded their share of the growing market for encaustic tiles, competing with increasing success against the Minton empire in Stoke-on-Trent. Designs suitable for domestic use such as on the hearth were developed; many were fresh, flowery subjects leaving behind the more strictly medieval revival. Maw & Co also set about developing brightly-coloured and strongly-patterned majolica tiles. They presented these at the 1862 International Exhibition, London. One of the principal features of the company's stand, devised by George Maw, was a chimney-piece of Maw's majolica tiles set in stone which was designed by Matthew Digby Wyatt. Its success opened the way for Maw & Co's eventual major share in the market for wall and fireplace tiles.

Maw & Co established their own design office, employing some locally trained talent from the Coalbrookdale School of Art, but they were shrewd enough from the outset to see the merit of commissioning designs from prominent architects (such as G E Street and George Goldie) as well as researching and reproducing historical designs themselves. In 1864 Walter Crane was employed to design a series of tiles based on nursery rhymes. Later, in the 1880s, Crane contributed designs for seven pieces of Maw's art pottery which attracted a good deal of attention for the firm at contemporary exhibitions.

The Maw family were great travellers and assiduously recorded tile designs and other decorative details on their journeys. Clearly, marble pavements from Italy provided inspiration for the later geometric arrangements of ceramic tiles which appeared in Maw's catalogues. The

Suggested arrangement for wall and floor tiles and faience from a Maw catalogue, c.1880.

surviving drawings include an extensive series executed in St Mary's Cathedral, Venice, in the summer of 1861. A later series, in 1863, covered the famous medieval tiles and mosaics *in situ* in Yorkshire abbeys. Thus, the manufacturing output of the firm, certainly until it became a limited liability company in 1888, was based on a background of sound scholarship by an informed and educated family.

The Maws were concerned with the technical aspects of tile-making too, and were granted over 20 patents during the 19th century. One of these was for a distinctive 'patent mosaic' whereby the mosaic 'pieces' were produced in tile form, separated by shallow grooves which were filled with cement when the tiles were laid, giving the random appearance of true mosaic work at a fraction of the cost. In complete contrast to such mechanical mass-production were the hand-painted lustre tiles which Maw's produced and displayed at the Arts and Crafts Exhibitions in the 1890s. Charles Henry Temple made an important contribution to the design output of the firm at this time and pioneered the decorative use of eggshell glazes.

Commercial success for Maw & Co in the second half of the 19th century was not without attendant problems. Expansion of their Benthall Works, Broseley, where they had steadily progressed since 1852, was physically limited by the steep nature of the valley. The outcome was the purchase of land at nearby Jackfield and the erection of a vast new Benthall Works, opened with great celebration on 10 May 1883 (denoted as 'BENTHALL WORKS, JACKFIELD' on back-marks). The architect for the new works was Charles Lynam of Stoke-on-Trent who had already designed tile works for Maw's rivals, Craven Dunnill and Minton Hollins. This was larger than both, with buildings covering two hectares, and represented the contemporary ultimate in sophisticated tile factory planning.

Although the fortunes of the company waned after World War I, some strong Art Deco designs were produced by in-house designers for use in bathrooms and on slabbed fireplaces of the 1930s. Tile production continued at Jackfield until 1969 by which time Maw & Co had become part of H & R Johnson-Richards Tiles Ltd who continue the company's name for tube-lined tiles produced today in Stoke-on-Trent. ⚘

Back-mark used on Maw tiles (c.1852–1860).

Select Bibliography

P Benthall 'George Maw: A Versatile Victorian' *National Trust Studies 1980*, Sotheby Parke Bernet, London 1979
M Messenger *Pottery and Tiles of the Severn Valley*, Remploy, London 1979

"...the output of Craven Dunnill closely followed their Shropshire rivals..."

CRAVEN DUNNILL TILES

Tony Herbert BSC DIP CONS
ADVISER ON HISTORIC TILES AND
ARCHITECTURAL CERAMICS

Craven Dunnill ruby lustre tile depicting a lion, c.1890. (Private collection.)

The Shropshire firm of Craven Dunnill & Co are frequently overshadowed historically by their larger rival, Maw & Co, who were located only a few hundred yards further down the River Severn at Jackfield, in the Ironbridge Gorge. Because of modern-day confusion with the tobacco firm of Dunhill, their name (without an 'h') is misspelt with depressing frequency even by such eminent writers as Nikolaus Pevsner.

Craven Dunnill evolved from a series of short-lived tile-making partnerships during the 1860s whose products (geometric and some patterned encaustic tiles) were marked with a confusing variety of names such as Hawes, Denny & Hargreaves and Hargreaves & Craven. In July 1870 a new company was formed (Hargreaves, Craven Dunnill Co) and during the following four years a large, well-planned and purpose-built tile works was erected. The architect was Charles Lynam who had then recently completed the Minton Hollins tile factory, Stoke-on-Trent.

Geometric and encaustic tiles formed the basis of production during the 1870s and '80s, using mainly local clay. These tiles were used to decorate arches above the windows in the new factory. Craven Dunnill produced a series of medieval encaustic designs which they described as their *Ancient* range. Derived from authentic sources and produced in a way which ensured a 'hand-made' look, these, along with their line-impressed tiles, became popular with church restoration architects such as George Gilbert Scott who despised the crisp, mechanical look of many contemporary 19th century encaustic tiles. Craven Dunnill made tiles for the restoration of both Chester and Bangor Cathedrals and also geometric tiles for dados at Manchester Town Hall, designed by Alfred Waterhouse.

By the 1890s wall tiles comprised a substantial part of the firm's output and this was extended into a range of glazed architectural faience. This latter included two patterns of ceramic bar fronts which became popular in late-19th century tiled public houses. There are surviving examples in the Gunmakers' Arms, Birmingham and the Crown Bar, Belfast. Hand-painted decoration of tiles paralleled many of the other major firms with a series of barbotine flower subjects (often on 6in x 12in tiles) having similarities with work by Burmantofts, Leeds. Large picture panels are not common, but the seven of scenery from the north east of England which survive at the Mountain Daisy Hotel, Sunderland, are particularly noteworthy. Another Craven Dunnill speciality in the same region was the series of tiled railway route maps produced for the North Eastern Railway, of which an example survives at York Station.

Although always smaller than Maw & Co, the output of Craven Dunnill closely followed their Shropshire rivals. Lustre decorated tiles were a particular speciality and included designs by Lewis F Day. Craven Dunnill are known to have supplied blank biscuit tiles to William De Morgan and with such an interest in art tiles it is perhaps not surprising to find they ventured into art pottery, too. A range of shaped tiles based on Alhambra patterns were produced and used in suitably exotic surroundings such as Turkish baths.

Many Craven Dunnill wall tiles bear the firm's distinctive back-mark which in both large and small versions incorporates a smoking bottle oven. Tile production ceased in the early-1950s but the firm continues as a tile distribution company based in Bridgnorth, Shropshire. The 1870s factory survives in a remarkably complete state and is now owned by the Ironbridge Gorge Museum. ❧

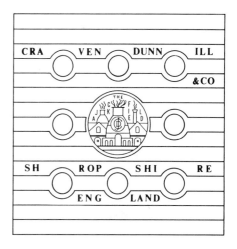

Back-mark used on Craven Dunnill tiles (c.1880–1910).

Select Bibliography

A T Herbert 'Jackfield Decorative Tiles in Use' *Industrial Archaeology Review* Vol 3 No 2, 1979

S Strachan 'Henry Powell Dunnill: A Victorian Tilemaster' *Journal of the Tiles & Architectural Ceramics Society*, Vol 3, 1990

"...Cream colour Tyle are much wanted,
& the consumption will be great..."

WEDGWOOD TILES

Gaye Blake-Roberts FMA FRSA
CURATOR
THE WEDGWOOD MUSEUM
STOKE-ON-TRENT

Design by Jane A Miles for 'September', from the set of 12 Wedgwood tiles depicting the months of the year. (Courtesy: Wedgwood.)

With the perfection of Queen's Ware, a fine cream-coloured earthenware body, by Josiah Wedgwood I and the desire of the aristocracy to incorporate various follies into their estates, Wedgwood realized the potential for the production of tiles. Wedgwood wrote to his friend Thomas Bentley in Liverpool: *'Cream colour Tyle are much wanted, & the consumption will be great for Dairys, Baths, Summer houses, Temples &c. &c. This Article will come under the Ornamental Class, & you may be looking out for a sober Tyle maker amongst your Potthouses to bring along with you'* (5 August 1767).

Many land owners created dairies specifically to include Wedgwood's creamware, *'Lady Gower will build a dairy on purpose to furnish it with cream couler (sic) if I will engaged to make Tiles for the Walls and many others I make no doubt will follow her example'* (17 September 1769). Other eminent people requested ceramics for their dairies including Warren Hastings at Daylesford House, near Moreton-in-Marsh, Gloucestershire, the Duke of Marlborough, the Duc d'Orléans and the Duke of Bedford for whom Henry Holland designed a delightful fantasy Chinese dairy completed in 1794.

Undoubtedly the best preserved set of 18th century Wedgwood tiles occur in a dairy design by Henry Holland for Lavinia, Countess of Spencer at Althorp, Northamptonshire. The modest single-storey building has tiled interior walls above wide, white marble shelves. Hand-painted enamel borders of ivy occur around the shelf, windows and frieze. Specific instructions were provided as to how to paint, 'pattern 486', ensuring that the design met properly at the corners. The standard wall tile was 7in square but the Countess requested hers to be 6in. For the painted tiles, Josiah quoted 1/- [5p] each but was cut down to 10d [4p], whilst the

Countess paid only 3d [1p] each for the 1,300 plain tiles she required. The whole was completed by 1787.

Other women, such as the Duchess of Argyll, required transfer-printed decoration on their tiles. This was handled in a slightly different way as Wedgwood's letters explain. The plain-glazed tiles went direct from Wedgwood to the customer; those to be printed were glazed by Wedgwood and sent to Liverpool. There, Guy Green added the over-glaze transfer-printed decoration and forwarded them to the customer from the port.

Apart from creamware tiles, Josiah Wedgwood I considered the production of decorative tiles for floors in his ornamental bodies, especially after the perfection of Jasper in 1774. He sent to Thomas Bentley in London, two year later, *'Patterns of Bricks for a Jasper floor 9 squares long by 6 broad, with a border of Porphyry and Black ones sufficient for one side and end. No. 1, 2 & 3 are first attempts for makeing Tiles for Baths &c. They will be made pretty expeditiously, & borders of different colors may be made to form them into compartments'* (26 January 1776).

During the early 19th century the consumption of tiles was not great. The largest order obtained between 1813 and 1834 was for 1,000 plain Queen's Ware tiles, but the manuscripts do indicate the production at that time of drab, marbled, lustre and under-glaze blue transfer-printed tiles. Small quantities of majolica and *émail ombrant* tiles were manufactured but not in the quantities made by other makers specializing in architectural ceramics. The ornamental tiles produced between 1875 and 1902 also encompassed, according to the company's catalogue of 1878, *'Encaustic tiles and Mosaic pavements, Tiles for hearths, jambs and wall decoration. Hand-painted Majolica, printed, embossed, enamelled and plain glazed tiles of every description'*.

The pattern books for Wedgwood's tile production survive with many of the design outlines printed out. These include the conventional florals through to abstract designs and the pictorial views which were introduced in March 1877. When Thomas Allen became Art Director in 1900, the number of tile designs rapidly increased, including many popular scenes such as *Ivanhoe, Banquet, Little Red Riding Hood, Greek Musicians* and *Aesop's Fables* amongst others. He also worked in close association with Helen J A Miles, a professional artist and illustrator, together producing some charming sets influenced by Kate Greenaway, including *Months* or *Early English, Playmate* and scenes from *A Midsummer Night's Dream*. Many of the typically Victorian animal subjects such as *Dogs' Heads* and *Horses' Heads* were adapted from paintings by Colonel Henry Hope Crealock, whilst a humorous set depicting fishing was taken from John Leech's cartoons published in *Punch*. Many of these tile patterns were adapted for the production of tablewares.

Design by Thomas Allen for a Wedgwood tile, c.1880. (Courtesy: Wedgwood.)

Another development was the introduction of the Marsden Patent Art Tile. In January 1880 George Anthony Marsden offered to Wedgwood his patent process for an *'Improvement in the Manufactory of Coloured or Ornamental Tiles, Bricks and other like Articles'*. An agreement was reached and trials began almost immediately. The first samples were sent to Wedgwood's London Manager, Charles Bachhoffner, to be shown to architects and builders. It was apparent that the initial designs were not striking enough although the architect Alfred Waterhouse was enthusiastic about the method, offering to give a pattern to the company for production. This encouraged Wedgwood to approach other designers and architects who supplied patterns for the range. One of the most significant designers was Lewis F Day. Production of Marsden Patent Tiles commenced towards the end of 1881 with a range of Day's stylized foliate designs.

In 1883 Wedgwood first employed a full-time traveller acting as an agent to sell their tiles. He acquired some valuable contracts including the Admiralty, the India Office, the Colonial Office, work for the Post Office, Harrogate Baths and various ship builders. By January 1890 Wedgwood was one of the founding members of the Tile Association, but as part of the general factory retrenchment at the end of the 19th century the agreement with Marsden was cancelled. Gradually the business declined further until October 1902 when the department was closed. ❧

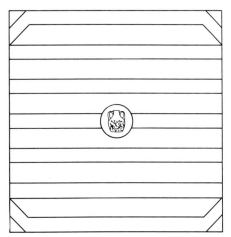

Back-mark used on Wedgwood tiles (c.1878–1900).

Select Bibliography

M Batkin *Wedgwood Ceramics 1846–1959*, Richard Dennis Publications, Shepton Beauchamp 1982
A Kelly *Decorative Wedgwood in Architecture and Furniture*, Born-Hawes Publishing, New York 1965
R Reilly *Wedgwood*, 2 Vols, Macmillan, London 1989
R Reilly & G Savage *The Dictionary of Wedgwood*, Antique Collectors' Club, Woodbridge 1980
G Wills *Wedgwood*, Country Life Books, London 1980

"...an excellent reputation for hand-painted pictorial tile murals..."

DOULTON TILES

The London firm of Doulton & Co was established in 1815 and quickly built up a reputation for good quality utilitarian stonewares. However, Henry Doulton, the son of the founder, recognized the more creative applications of their salt-glazed stoneware medium and, encouraged by the principal of the local School of Art, John Sparkes, set up a studio in Lambeth producing art pottery and sculpture as well as tiles and terracotta for architectural purposes.

By the late-1870s Doulton's trade catalogues were full of ceramic building components and a variety of carved and moulded tile designs in salt-glazed stoneware. As this technique involved firing to very high temperatures the resulting tiles were impervious to damp and atmospheric corrosion and so were particularly suitable for outside locations. A number of examples can still be seen *in situ* at the surviving art studio building in Lambeth High Street which was built in 1878 and served as a three-dimensional catalogue for passing architects. Many important commissions for Doulton tiles ensued, the most splendid being the vestibule at Lloyds Bank, Strand, London, formerly the Palsgrove Hotel. Leading Lambeth stoneware artists were involved in the design of such schemes under the supervision of Art Director, Wilton P Rix.

Individual stoneware tiles were also produced for incorporation in furniture, notably the animal designs by Hannah Barlow, the studio's first woman artist. The best known example of her work is the cabinet by Gillow & Co which was shown at the International Exhibition, London, 1872, and is now in the Victoria and Albert Museum.

It was more usual to decorate furniture with colourful earthenware tiles and Doulton's faience department specialized in painting tiles to

Louise Irvine MA (HONS)
ROYAL DOULTON HISTORIAN

Doulton fireplace panels painted by Florence Lewis, c.1885. (Courtesy: Phillips.)

Doulton fairytale panel designed by William Rowe for the Lilian Ward, St Thomas's Hospital, London, opened in 1901. (Courtesy: Royal Doulton Ltd.)

enhance cabinets, flower boxes, washstands, fireplace surrounds and also the patent radiating tile stoves which incorporated a wide range of designs. Most of the faience painters were recruited from the Lambeth School of Art and initially they were trained by John Bennett, who was instrumental in developing Doulton's faience-painting technique. He was also responsible for the decoration of some of the early tiles but, in 1877, he emigrated to the USA where he set up his own studio pottery. Fortunately, he had an able successor in Florence Lewis who continued his role as instructor to the new artists and tile decorators.

The subject matter of the faience tiles was extremely varied and included figure studies, flowers, landscapes, birds and animals. In the 1880s individual tiles could be purchased from 1/2d [6p] to 32/6d [£1.52¹/₂] depending on the size and degree of complexity in colour and design. It is interesting to note that the most expensive tiles cost considerably more than the decorator's weekly wage.

Many of Doulton's earliest faience tiles feature the monogram of Helen J A Miles, the prolific painter and book illustrator who also produced tile designs for Wedgwood. Other artists associated with the development of Doulton tiles included Katherine Sturgeon, who was a figurative painter; Alberta Green, who is known to have painted some aesthetic style portrait heads; Linnie Watts and Ada Dennis, who both specialized in rustic scenes populated with children; and Margaret Challis and Josephine Durtnall, who concentrated on floral designs.

Usually the faience artists painted tiles which had been bought in from other manufacturers such as Minton Hollins or Craven Dunnill and the Doulton factory mark was added to the back on completion of the design. However, Doulton did manufacture an earthenware tile with a 'patent safety back' and the extra adhesive qualities of this design were promoted in a catalogue of 1880. These tiles were used in some of the 19th century studio's largest commissions; for example, the decoration of the Indian apartments at the Cecil Hotel, London, which required thousands of hand-painted tiles in Indian designs, and the Birkbeck Bank, London, which was clad inside and out with Doulton's architectural ceramics. The crowning glory of this extraordinary building was the huge dome in the banking hall which featured 16 large tile panels representing trades and industries connected with banking. The Doulton studio had an excellent reputation for hand-painted pictorial tile murals such as these. John Eyre was usually responsible for the design and several different artists were involved in the painting depending on the subject matter. John McLennan was famed for his portraiture, Walter Nunn favoured historical and theatrical tableaux and Esther Lewis was the best landscape painter. Their combined talents enlivened public houses such as the Café Royal, Edinburgh, the dining rooms of private residences such as Queen Alexandra's House, London, and even a gentlemen's public convenience in Paisley, Scotland.

At the turn of the century the faience studio artists began to specialize in a new style of tile mural for children's hospitals, featuring nursery rhymes and fairy tales, to make the young patients' enforced stay more enjoyable. William Rowe and Margaret Thompson designed several series of panels for hospitals all over Britain and as far afield as Poonah, India, and Wellington, New Zealand. The advantages of tiles for hospital decoration were extolled in a little book *Pictures in Pottery*, published by Doulton in 1904. Apart from being hygienic, the book claimed, tiles could bring *'light and reflections into even the darkest corners'*. Unfortunately, this glittering effect was considered detrimental by many architects and so Doulton overcame the problem by developing Vitreous Fresco, a non-reflective enamel-glazed tile particularly suitable for church interiors, and Parian ware which had an eggshell-like finish. This latter technique was perfected by William J Neatby who was head of Doulton's architectural department from 1890 to 1907. Neatby used it extensively in his decorative schemes, the most famous being Harrods food halls, built in 1901.

Doulton continued to produce tiling for Harrods after World War I and the art studio was still busy with tile commissions during the 1930s. Their largest ever undertaking was the tiling of Singapore Station in 1935. Eighteen huge tile panels depicting local industries, each nearly 24 feet high, were designed by William Rowe, creating some 2,000 square feet of tiling which was all painted by hand. Fortunately, this scheme remains intact and can be enjoyed by adventurous travellers. Many schemes also still survive in Britain and generally speaking they provide the best opportunity for the study of Doulton's expertise in architectural ceramics as their individual tiles are very rare and not often found in public or private collections. ❧

Select Bibliography

P Atterbury & L Irvine *The Doulton Story,* Royal Doulton Tableware Ltd, Stoke-on-Trent 1979

C Braithwaite *Phillips Collector's Guide to Royal Doulton,* Boxtree, London 1989

Royal Doulton *Pictures in Pottery,* Royal Doulton Potteries, London 1904

Back-mark used on Doulton tiles (c.1890–1900).

"...to us pattern designers, Persia has become a Holy Land..."

Morris & Co and William De Morgan Tiles

Jon Catleugh
Architect
Trustee of the De Morgan
Foundation

William De Morgan ruby lustre tile depicting a pelican painted on a commercial blank, c.1875. (Private collection.)

Contrary to popular belief, William Morris did not excel in all fields of design and some materials did not seem to interest him as much as others. Many people would claim that he was the greatest pattern designer of the 19th century when it came to wallpapers and printed and woven textiles, but he did comparatively little designing for stained glass and tiles and none for furniture. He was a visionary who saw what needed to be done to improve the world both socially and aesthetically and he was fortunate to have talented friends who could carry out those ideas in the areas where he had less interest or just not enough time to do it himself. To think of him as a design impresario in no way diminishes his stature. Artists and friends who provided designs for tiles included Edward Burne-Jones, D G Rossetti, Ford Madox Brown, Albert Moore, Simeon Soloman, Philip Webb, Kate and Lucy Faulkner and, of course, William De Morgan.

There was something slightly amateur about Morris & Co's tile production. There were obvious technical shortcomings: failing colours that went beyond the normally acceptable irregularities of hand craftwork, disintegrating glazes, blues that turned out to be grey, or at best, grey-green, and other discolourations; some tile panels installed in St Peter's, Bournemouth, Dorset, in the 1870s had to be replaced in 1899 because the glaze had turned to powder and the designs had totally disappeared. In the early days of Morris & Co tiles were fired in a muffle kiln (with the firm's stained glass) at temperatures that were too low for ideal results. It is hardly surprising that Morris handed over the production of his tiles to more proficient producers in Holland and De Morgan took over production of some designs but with modifications.

A distinction must always be made between the technically amateur and what at first sight might appear to be pictorially amateur. There are a number of story-telling series (*Beauty and the Beast*, *Cinderella*, *Sleeping Beauty*, *Legend of Good Women*, etc.) that were deliberately simple – the techniques of tile painting demanded it – and have a delightful naïve quality that suits the stories and accords with the Morrisian vision of the Middle Ages. Whether it was aesthetically sound to carry out small paintings on tiles and incorporate them into architecture is debatable. Morris said in a lecture that things done in pottery should be logical to the material and technique in a way that could only be done in pottery. In these pictorial tiles he allowed his designers to move away from strict rules, but Morris's principles were applied in almost all other designs made by the firm – designs to fill the space, no illusion of a third dimension, simple repeating diaper patterns, always hand painted and never printed or stencilled.

Morris & Co designs produced in Holland can be a trap for tile collectors; many Dutch-made tiles are circulating as having been *made* by the firm. As Morris-made tiles were painted on plain, white-glazed tiles imported from Holland, the design lay on top of the glaze unlike the tiles made in Holland which were invariably in-glaze painted; a glance along the surface of the tile against the light will usually show whether it is in-glaze or over-glaze. Also, many designs made in Holland were *in the style* of Morris, or at least in a generalized Arts and Crafts style and have often been confused with genuine Morris & Co designs. The firm confused the issue by stocking Dutch 'Morris style' designs in their Oxford Street, London, shop.

Apart from the pictorial tiles already mentioned, there were other typical designs: single flower clumps (*Daisy*, *Columbine*, etc., based on the *Daisy* wallpaper) by Morris; birds and animals by Philip Webb and diaper repeat patterns by Kate Faulkner. Morris himself designed some figures that were used in stained glass as well as on tiles; an economical concept because if they had wings attached they could be used as angels and when they carried instruments they were musicians. Morris also designed three tiles for De Morgan and they too were sold at the Oxford Street shop.

The eclectic tastes of the early Victorians were based principally on a knowledge of Gothic and Classical themes often as interpreted by the artists of the Italian Renaissance, but new forces were at work. Pugin was appalled by the decline of standards of design since the Middle Ages and preached a return to what he believed were the 'true principles'. Many others (John Ruskin, F D Maurice *et al*) followed but none more passionately than William Morris. The supremacy of hand craftsmanship and socialism were the bases of Morris's 'alternative society'.

Willian De Morgan tile depicting the 'Bedford Park anemone', painted in pale manganese mauve and green. Sands End back-mark, c.1888–97. (Private collection.)

Islamic design was virtually unknown in Britain and when Indian artifacts were exhibited at the Crystal Palace, in 1851, their novelty and quality amazed the design world. Owen Jones, involved in the organization of the Great Exhibition, had already made a study of Moorish architecture and decoration and had published (1842–54) spectacular colour lithographs of the Alhambra. His *Grammar of Ornament* (1856) illustrated patterns and motifs from all over the world and from many centuries. The arts of Persia, Turkey, India, Moorish Spain and Africa were available for study and formed the core of the exhibits in the newly founded Museum of Manufactures (1852) later to become the Victoria and Albert Museum, London.

William De Morgan first met William Morris and Edward Burne-Jones in 1863, and was immediately absorbed into the 'never-never world' that Morris and his circle believed to have been the way life was in the Middle Ages. De Morgan had been trained as a painter at the Academy Schools but, realizing his limitations, started to design stained glass, tiles and painted furniture for Morris's firm. Morris was enthusiastic about the Persian and Turkish exhibits being purchased for the South Kensington Museum (in a lecture published in 1882 he said, *'to us pattern designers, Persia has become a Holy Land'*) and much of his enthusiasm must have rubbed off on De Morgan because many of his earliest designs showed a knowledge of Isnik patterns. De Morgan found that the dictatorial control that Morris had over all the designers working for him was inhibiting and in 1869 he set up his own studio in Fitzroy Square, London.

Between 1870 and 1872 De Morgan experimented with lustre glazes on tiles. This happened more or less by accident when he noticed that silver used in the painting of outlines on his glass produced an iridescent effect when fired and he believed, quite rightly, that a similar effect could be achieved with tiles. Lustre glazes were probably first used in Egypt in the 9th century and they reached a peak at Kashan (Persia) in the 13th century. Knowledge of the technique travelled across North Africa into Moorish Spain and reached Italy (Deruta, Gubbio, Faenza, etc.) in the 15th century. The iridescent or oil-on-water effect of lustre is the result of a microscopically thin film of metal deposited by reduction in the kiln. It is interesting to note that lustre must have been 'waiting to be discovered' because others were doing similar experimental work quite unknown to each other at the same time: Théodore Deck at Sèvres, Clément Massier at Golfe-Juan (near Cannes) and Ulisse Cantagalli (from 1878–1902) in Florence. De Morgan's other rediscovery were the blue and green glazes that he called his 'Persian colours', but they were, in fact, the colours used at Isnik in the 16th century at the peak of Ottoman tile-making.

William De Morgan tile depicting a ship painted in monochrome green. Sands End back-mark, c.1888–97. (Private collection.)

De Morgan's designs fall into three broad categories: those influenced by Morris's imagery of simple English flowers as depicted in herbals and manuscripts; those that clearly are derived from Isnik sources; and figurative designs such as ships, birds and animals (real and fantastic). The total number is not known but there are 1,248 sheets of his designs for tiles, tile panels, pots and dishes in the Victoria and Albert Museum. Many tiles exist for which no drawings are known and many drawings do not appear to have been made into tiles.

The dating of his tiles can be simple because after he started to make his own tile bodies (*c*.1872) he impressed his name on the back, changing the design of the impression frequently as and when he moved from Chelsea to Merton Abbey or when he moved to Sands End, Fulham. Dating the designs is a more difficult problem because many designs proved good sellers and were in production over many years, some from *c*.1870 until he closed the pottery in 1907. Many of his designs were made in several different colours. For instance, the animal and ship tiles can be found in blue, green or red lustre; some ships are in polychrome and some animals produced at the end of his career were made in polychrome with two or three colour lustres on the same tile, technically extremely difficult to make. Most of the flower designs were made with yellow, blue or pink flowers. The Isnik inspired designs usually observed the Isnik palettes.

After De Morgan ceased work as a potter he took to writing fiction and before his death in 1917 he had published seven best-selling novels (his wife completed the eighth after his death). Both De Morgan and Evelyn, his wife, were active supporters of the Suffragette Movement and were pacifists, so it is a sad irony that he met his death from trench fever caught from a friend visiting him while on leave from France in 1917. ❧

Select Bibliography

J Catleugh *William De Morgan Tiles*, Trefoil , London 1983
W G Gaunt & M D E Clayton-Stamm *William De Morgan*, Studio Vista, London 1971
M Greenwood *Designs of William De Morgan*, Richard Dennis, Shepton Beauchamp 1989

Catalogues
Painted Tiles to be had of William De Morgan at Orange House Pottery, (privately
        published) 1880
Catalogue of Works by William De Morgan, Victoria and Albert Museum, London 1921

Sands End back-mark used on William De Morgan tiles (c.1888–97).

PILKINGTON TILES

Deborah Skinner BA AMA
CERAMICS SECTION
CITY MUSEUM & ART GALLERY
STOKE-ON-TRENT

Detail from a six-tile Pilkington panel of the 1930s depicting a foundry worker. Semi-matt glaze with design painted in shades of green. (City Museum & Art Gallery, Stoke-on-Trent.)

In common with a number of other art tile and pottery manufacturers, Pilkington's flourished outside the traditional pottery-making areas. The venture was established as a result of the discovery of good quality brick-making marl during mining operations at Clifton Junction, Swinton, near Manchester.

The resounding success of the company, which began production of tiles and pottery only very late in the 19th century, was due to two principal factors: the entrepreneurial skills of the proprietors, the Pilkington brothers and their securing the services of talented managers and staff, and massive public demand for decorative tiles and the prevailing taste for design styles such as Art Nouveau which was eminently suited to tile and pottery decoration. The commissioning of designs from leading figures in the contemporary art world such as Walter Crane, C F A Voysey and Lewis F Day ensured that Pilkington's tiles and Royal Lancastrian art pottery were amongst the most stylish available in a highly competitive market.

Following the discovery of the marl, investigations were made into the possibility of manufacturing bricks, but after consultation with William Burton, a ceramic chemist with Josiah Wedgwood & Sons in the Potteries area of north Staffordshire, tile-making was settled upon as being more economically viable. In 1891 Pilkington's Tile & Pottery Co was formed and Burton himself employed as manager from 1892. In 1895 he was joined by his brother, Joseph, and together the Burton brothers were responsible for the early development of the company. Another important figure in the success of Pilkington's was Gordon Forsyth who joined the company in 1905 as Art Director, having previously worked in the same capacity for the

Stoke firm of Minton, Hollins & Co, where he designed tiles, faience and mosaics. He steered Pilkington's to the fore in the design field during his years with the company until his return to Stoke-on-Trent in 1920 to become Superintendent of Art Education.

The Pilkington company is well-known for its Royal Lancastrian art pottery with its dazzling and innovative glaze effects and lustres, but it is with the more extensive tile productions with which we are concerned here. Manufacture began in January 1893 using the local red clay, but after a time it was necessary to produce a more refined body and white-firing clays were brought in mainly from the south-west of England along with other raw materials. The majority of tiles were made by the dust-pressing technique, although where the decoration required it, a plastic body was used. Decorative techniques included a full range of printing, painting, tube-lining and relief moulding, with particularly fine results being achieved by the use of coloured glazes developed by the factory chemists, used in conjunction with relief moulded or tube-lined patterns and scenes from leading designers. The company concentrated mainly on tiles for walls, hearths and furniture, with some specially produced murals and decorative panels. The international exhibitions provided an excellent platform for this trade and Pilkington's won acclaim at many such events including the Winnipeg Industrial Exhibition (1898); the Paris Exhibition (1900) where designs by Walter Crane, Lewis F Day and C F A Voysey were shown; the Glasgow Exhibition (1901) at which four panels based on the designs *Les Fleurs* by Alphonse Mucha were displayed, and the Franco-British Exhibition (1908) when two leading contemporary architects, Edgar Wood and J M Sellars, designed the Pilkington's trade stand. Among the company's major commissions were tiles inspired by Isnik designs for the transatlantic liner *Titanic*, panels depicting pottery through the ages designed by Gordon Forsyth in 1914 for the City of Liverpool Museums (destroyed in demolition work following bomb damage during World War II) and painted tile murals for Maypole Dairies, Lancashire.

At Pilkington's, the decorative styles adapted for use on tiles were generally in keeping with prevalent taste: the Isnik or Persian-influenced designs of John Chambers and Gordon Forsyth were reminiscent of the work of William De Morgan, whilst the Art Nouveau designs of Walter Crane, C F A Voysey, Lewis F Day and others were particularly fine examples of this style which was adopted wholesale with varying degrees of success by almost all the major tile manufacturers. Lustres, also popularized by De Morgan, were used on tiles in a more limited way, as were glaze effects such as *rouge flambé*, but their use was generally restricted

Detail from a cartoon for a Pilkington tile panel, 'Persian 800–1600 AD'. From a series depicting pottery through the ages by Gordon Forsyth for the City of Liverpool Museums, 1914. Panel size 15ft x 8ft. (City Museum & Art Gallery, Stoke-on-Trent.)

to art pottery. Pictorial and illustrative tiles were a popular part of the company's production while plain-glazed tiles made up the bread-and-butter output, particularly during the 1920s–'50s period when matt and mottled glazes for bathroom, kitchen and fireplace tiles enjoyed widespread popularity.

Following the retirement of William Burton in 1915 and the departure of Gordon Forsyth in 1920, innovation in the art pottery department slowed down and in 1938 this part of the production ceased. However, art pottery as a percentage of overall production may never have been much above ten per cent, so the fortunes of the company were related primarily to tile production. In 1937 the title Pilkington's Tiles Ltd was adopted and subsequently, having survived the economic difficulties of the 1930s and World War II, business prospered. In 1964, Carter & Co, tile manufacturers at Poole, Dorset, and Pilkington's merged to form the company of Pilkington & Carter, although the new firm very soon reverted to the Pilkington's title which continues today. The present company successfully produces good quality tiles for the building and DIY industries in the face of stiff competition from abroad. ✤

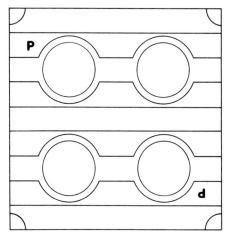

Back-mark used on Pilkington tiles (c.1892–1910).

Select Bibliography

A J Cross *Pilkington's Royal Lancastrian Pottery and Tiles*, Richard Dennis Publications, London 1980
A Lomax *Royal Lancastrian Pottery 1900–1938*, A Lomax (privately published), Bolton 1957

"...research has been undertaken to identify the manufacturers..."

TILES FROM THE BACK

People often ask about a Victorian tile, *'Who made it?'* More fully, there are at least two questions: *'Who made the blank?'* and *'Who decorated it?'*. Although the answer to both questions is frequently the same, there were quite substantial companies, most notably the Decorative Art Tile Co, who decorated blanks purchased from other major manufacturers. Moreover, manufacturers occasionally purchased blanks from their rivals, possibly if they had insufficient stocks of their own.

Although many manufacturers such as Minton & Co, Minton, Hollins & Co and Maw & Co used their name or initials moulded or impressed into the reverse of their tiles, many others did not. Even those that did also made use of 'anonymous' backplates. In the last few years considerable research has been undertaken to identify the manufacturers and decorators of these unmarked tiles.

One major source of information has come from the investigation of registered designs. Companies could gain legal protection against designs being copied by registering them with the Board of Trade, and these registers are still held at the Public Records Office at Kew. Prior to 1884 designs so protected carried a 'diamond' registration mark which contained in coded form the date of registration, the 'class' (metal, wood, pottery, fabric, etc.) and a 'parcel number' which identified a particular register entry. From February 1884 a simple registration number was used.

When a tile or other object bearing such a mark is found the register can be checked to identify the person or company registering the design. Most usually this is the manufacturer and so an anonymous blank can then be identified. However, some caution is needed as occasionally

Peter Clegg
RESEARCHER INTO TILE BACKS
AND TILE REGISTRATION MARKS

Tile back showing the name of the maker (Minton's China Works), the place of manufacture (Stoke-on-Trent), the country of origin (England), the Minton trade mark (globe), the catalogue pattern number (2684) and the registration number (219706) for the year 1884.

designs were registered by a freelance designer such as Thomas Elphick, the architect, or by an ironfounder or large retailer for exclusive use in their products which they might then have manufactured and decorated by a variety of manufacturers. Designs registered to tile decorators, of course, reveal who decorated the tile, but not who manufactured the blank.

A second source of information are manufacturers' catalogues or pattern books. If one can find a design on an unknown blank in one of these it is usually reasonable to assume that one has found the maker or decorator. Some care is again needed, however, as some designs seem to appear in several different catalogues and some manufacturers seem to have purchased or 'pirated' the rights to designs from companies which went out of business.

Once the process of identification has started other clues proliferate. Many companies, for example, used distinctive pattern numbers or other marks. Sherwin & Cotton pattern numbers, for their transfer-printed designs at least, used three or four digits preceded by an S; the Marsden Tile Co seems to have used some sort of rubber stamp with the pattern number starting with a G or K; Wood & Co used literary names rather than numbers: *Tennyson, Keats, Wordsworth* and so on; many T & R Boote transfer designs have a printed HP on the reverse; and there are many other examples.

If one finds identical designs on a known and unknown blank then, again, attributing both to the same manufacturer seems reasonable. However, as we have already observed some designs were manufactured by several companies. One needs to examine the two examples carefully to ensure that the same transfer or moulding was used in both cases.

In other cases examination of known reverses reveals some common feature in the manufacturing process. For example, Gibbons Hinton used a wide variety of reverses, but all had a groove into which the pattern number was slid and held in place by a distinctive 'lock'. It seems reasonable to assume that other reverses using this lock can, therefore, be attributed to Gibbons Hinton.

Finally, several companies used distinctive decorative techniques, for example the stencil and airbrush technique used by Woolliscroft for their own tiles and those made for Derwent Foundry, or Gibbons Hinton's Chromo-Relievo tiles. Where examples of these techniques are found on unknown reverses an attribution can again be made.

One difficulty in identification is that although most manufacturers did 'personalize' their backplates in some way – a letter, a distinctive style of pattern numbers, etc. – some used backplates as supplied by the tile

Back-mark used on T & R Boote tiles, (c.1862–1910).

press manufacturer. One example of this is a barré reverse with five raised bars and sunken quarter circle corners. Pilkington's used this reverse but with a P stamped in two diagonally opposite corners; Lea & Boulton used the same reverse with LT stamped into the backplate above the central bar; a Marsden example has a crudely cut X and a small circle; but who manufactured the version without any marks at all?

To confuse the issue further, there is now evidence that manufacturers occasionally purchased second-hand presses from each other. Thus, J H Barratt used a heavily modified backplate originally used by Wedgwood, and there is some evidence that when George Anthony Marsden left Wedgwood, he may have taken presses with him and worked briefly for Doulton before setting up his own company, again using the same presses.

The study of reverses also reveals a degree of pride or otherwise shown by manufacturers. Decorative Art Tile Co went so far as to register a reverse showing a stork and rising sun (Rd No 271234: 18 February 1896). From W Godwin's impressed reverse complete with Welsh dragon and the motto 'INVICTAE FIDELITATIS PROEMIUM' ('the reward of faithfulness unconquered') on some of their early encaustics or Craven Dunnill's proud 'badge' of their Jackfield site, through the anonymous but immaculately machined reverses of T G & F Booth to the frankly scruffy and poorly modelled reverses of Woolliscroft, the range is surprising. ❧

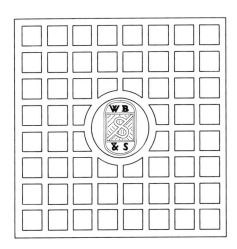

Back-mark used on W B Simpson tiles, (c.1880–1900).

Select Bibliography

J & B Austwick *The Decorated Tile*, Pitman House, London 1980
P & D Clegg 'Back Chat' articles in *Glazed Expressions*, Tiles & Architectural
    Ceramics Society *from* 1983

> *"...most homes had cast-iron fireplaces with tiles on either side of the grate..."*

TILES AND INTERIOR FURNISHINGS

Hans van Lemmen DIP ART ATC BA
SENIOR LECTURER IN ART AND
DESIGN HISTORY
LEEDS POLYTECHNIC

'The Mountain Daisy', Sunderland, c.1895. Craven Dunnill mosaic floor, wall tiles with landscape panels and ceramic bar front.

Tiles were not only used on walls and floors, but were also incorporated in interior furnishings. Tiles can often be seen as part of fireplaces and stoves as well as certain items of furniture. In this context, tiles can be studied socially as the quality of the tiles and the furnishings of which they are an integral part reflect the status of the owner.

Traditionally, tiles have been part of the fireplace because they are fireproof, reflect the heat into the room and can be cleaned easily. The Dutch, for example, used delftware tiles on a large scale in this way and in the 18th century this also became fashionable in Britain. In the 19th century, with the increasing use of cast-iron grates in Britain, tiles were frequently part of the structure. By the end of the 19th century most homes had cast-iron fireplaces with tiles on either side of the grate and immediately in front of the hearth. We only have to look at catalogues of iron works such as The Coalbrookdale Company or Barnard, Bishop & Barnard to see grates advertised with a choice of tiles to match. Not only the grate received tiles. Elaborate overmantels were constructed in which tiles were used for decorative reasons.

Tiles in furniture were used for functional as well as purely decorative reasons. The French produced some splendid cabinets and writing desks inlaid with Sèvres porcelain plaques for an exclusive clientele during the second half of the 18th century. Wedgwood did something similar at this time for the English market as some of Thomas Sheraton's furniture shows. Jasper ware cameos and medallions were produced as furniture decoration showing classical figures designed by John Flaxman. They were all expensive pieces, however, for a privileged section of society.

The fashion for tiles in 19th century furniture was encouraged by the examples seen at international exhibitions from 1851 onwards. Elaborate exhibition pieces were created by firms such as Jackson & Graham and Wright & Mansfield using Minton tiles and Wedgwood plaques, while Charles Bevan designed some fine pieces using Doulton tiles. Queen Victoria was fond of tiled furniture judging by the pieces made for Osborne House, Isle of Wight, around the middle of the century, but more humble lines of tiled furniture followed to satisfy the general market.

The mass-production of tiles after 1840 went hand-in-hand with the manufacture of factory-produced furniture for a buoyant middle-class market. The use of tiles in furniture was recognized. In the *Furniture Gazette* of 26 April 1879 we read, *'We recommend our cabinet making firms to introduce tiles wherever they can consistently do so'*. Tiles were applied across a range of different types of furniture. They were most frequently used in wash-stands, but they also found a place in hall-stands, umbrella-stands and hall chairs. In the living room there were tiled jardinières as well as the occasional tiled sideboard or wall cupboard. Tile manufacturers were well aware of this potential market. Maw & Co produced what they called *'faience furniture inlays'*, George Wooliscroft & Son made *'tiles for cabinet work'* and Minton, Hollins & Co advertised in their trade catalogues that *'Tiles are now in frequent use for inlaying in the panels of Cabinets, Sideboard, Hall Stands and in the Backs of Wash-tables &c'*. This fashion for tiles continued until World War I when there was a general decline. The inter-war period saw more utilitarian furniture which relied less on decoration.

There were exceptions however. The firm of Packard & Ord, Marlborough, Wiltshire, produced an interesting range of hand-painted tiles from the late 1930s onwards. During the early 1950s they had their tiles made up into all sorts of items, such as tiled tables, trays, flower boxes, tables and wall light fittings.

During the 1980s, renewed interest in Victorian design and Art Nouveau has led to the production of replica fireplaces and furniture together with reproductions of Victorian and Art Nouveau tiles. In a small way, history has turned full circle. ❧

Select Bibliography

A Kelly *Decorative Wedgwood in Architecture and Furniture*, Country Life, London 1965
H van Lemmen *Tiled Furniture*, Shire Publications, Princes Risborough 1989

Oak hall chair with a Minton's China Works tile designed by John Moyr Smith from the 'Shakespeare' series, c.1880. (Private collection.)

ARCHITECTURAL CERAMICS

Michael Stratton PHD
PROGRAMME DIRECTOR
THE IRONBRIDGE INSTITUTE
IRONBRIDGE GORGE MUSEUM

Craven Dunnill commemorative faience plaque from the Kardomah Café, Liverpool, 1905. (Now altered.)

The role of tiles in providing dramatic decoration in two dimensions was complemented by the brightly coloured and richly moulded forms of terracotta and its glazed derivative, faience. These materials, made up of large blocks of clay, were widely used in towns and cities during the Victorian period and the early-20th century. They offered potential for creating decorative façades that could resist the effects of soot and smoke, and at lower cost than comparable work in stonemasonry.

The earliest expressive use of terracotta in Britain dates to the Tudor period. During the early-16th century a group of artists produced ornaments for windows, screens and tombs in East Anglian churches, while the gateway to Hampton Court was enriched with roundels set with the heads of Roman Emperors.

Although most terracotta is bright red or buff in colour, the earliest stage of the revival of the material involved pressing and firing clays from the west of England to imitate the colour and texture of stone. Coade stone was made at Lambeth, London, from 1769, the bulk of the output of the Artificial Stone Manufactory being in the form of neo-Classical ornaments. Other, competing firms emerged, John Rossi producing four caryatids for St Pancras Church, London, 1818–22.

The Coade factory closed in 1839. In the same year construction commenced on the first building to make a more obviously 'Victorian' use of terracotta. Christ Church, Welshpool, was designed by Thomas Penson; in this and several other of his designs for churches in Welsh border towns he used yellow moulded bricks and terracotta for decorative detailing. While Penson's work received little contemporary attention, Edmund

Sharpe's Lancashire churches became a widely publicized test for the architectural use of terracotta. St Stephen's at Lever Bridge, Bolton, was built in 1842–5 with the walls, windows and even the pulpit, the organ and the pew ends made in ceramic. The High Church group, the Ecclesiologists, condemned this *'cast-clay church'*, and their opposition was enough to set back the revival of the material for a decade.

Terracotta gained an artistic and practical justification through its widespread use in the cultural complex of South Kensington, the art school and museum being funded from the profits of the Great Exhibition of 1851. During the early 1860s decorative artists, led by Godfrey Sykes, designed the ornamental columns and panels installed around the quadrangle of the Victoria and Albert Museum. The artists were based within the art school; by dispensing with the services of architects and stonemasons, rich decoration was achieved at a remarkably modest price.

The bulk of the terracotta for the Victoria and Albert Museum was supplied by Blanchard of Bishop's Waltham, Hampshire. The material for the Royal Albert Hall, built 1867–71, came from Gibbs & Canning of Tamworth, Staffordshire. Factories based on the coalfields came to dominate the market, benefiting from extensive resources of clay, while coal from the same mines was used to fire the kilns. The Natural History Museum, also supplied by Gibbs & Canning and completed in 1881, marked the high-point of the Victorian revival of terracotta. Alfred Waterhouse's masterpiece was clad, both inside and out, in buff and blue-grey blocks with images of lions, monkeys and dodos providing instruction and inspiration to visitors and curators alike.

Waterhouse exerted a dominating influence over the use of terracotta for the rest of the 19th century. He used bright red blocks, typically made at Ruabon, North Wales, for a series of offices for the Prudential·Assurance Co, of which the most notable is the London head office at Holborn, developed in stages from 1878. In 1886 Waterhouse judged the competition to choose the design for the Victoria Law Courts in Birmingham. The winning composition, by Aston Webb and Ingress Bell mixed red material for the exterior and buff for the lining of the main hall and corridors, all in a free Tudor Gothic style laden with sculpture conveying images of truth and justice. Birmingham was just one industrial city to gain numerous commercial and public buildings in terracotta. The skyline of the inner suburbs is dominated by Martin & Chamberlain's libraries and board schools, with traceried windows and soaring ventilation towers. Leeds gained a series of dramatic arcades, the grandest being the County Arcade designed by Frank Matcham in 1900.

Terracotta statue of Josiah Wedgwood, panels for the months of the year and the processes of pottery manufacture on the Wedgwood Institute, Burslem, Stoke-on-Trent. Modelled by R Morris, R Edgar and W Wright, produced by Blanchard & Co, London and Blashfield, Stamford, Lincolnshire, 1863–73.

The take-up of architectural ceramics in a city depended on the level of investment in new buildings, prevailing local tastes and the proximity of major manufacturers. William Watkins used terracotta on most of his commissions in Lincoln; Gunton of Costessey found a ready market for their Tudor-style chimney pots in Norwich; while the economic boom in lowland Lancashire, fuelled by coal and cotton, resulted in the extensive use of locally made ceramics in Preston, Wigan and St Helens. Manchester remained essentially a city of stone until Charles Trubshaw used material made by Leeds Fireclay for the Midland Hotel in 1898 and Whitworth Street was developed in the Edwardian period with terracotta warehouses.

London had only one major manufacturer, Doulton of Lambeth, but the enthusiasm of the capital's major estate owner, the Duke of Westminster, resulted in terracotta spreading across Mayfair during the 1880s and '90s. Mount Street is lined with prestigious apartment blocks with scrolls, cartouches, dolphins and cherubs moulded in a pale buff or salmon-coloured terracotta that forms the hallmark of Doulton's output.

Away from the commercial streets of towns and cities, simple window mouldings, pier caps and finials were used to enliven the frontages of terraces and villas. Houses close to a terracotta factory might often show an exuberant use of such decoration; suburban ceramics can be seen at their richest at Wrexham, Poole, Cleethorpes and Accrington. Textile mills, railway stations, public houses, blacksmith's shops, chapels and parrot houses were among the building types to be given red or buff moulded dressings, whether in an urban or rural setting.

Bright red terracotta passed out of fashion by the Edwardian period, but architectural ceramics were given a new lease of life through interest in polychromy and the technical capability to apply frost-resistant glazes to large blocks of clay. Glazed terracotta is generally known as 'faience'.

Some of the earliest uses of faience are to be found on the outside of the lecture block and in the refreshment room of the Victoria and Albert Museum. In the 1880s faience was used as an adjunct to tiling to line a number of London restaurants. In the following decade the same combination of materials was specified for public house interiors, arcades and the entrance halls of major public buildings. The head of the architectural department at Doulton, W J Neatby, designed the faience for three innovative examples of faience architecture: the Royal Arcade, Norwich (1899), the Turkish Café, Leicester (1890) and the Everard Building, Bristol (1901).

Rich colours and Art Nouveau detailing failed to appeal to mainstream architectural and public taste. Most Edwardian faience was

Salt-glazed terracotta chimney pot from Leeds, c.1900.

moulded with Classical detailing and dipped in cream or grey glazes. Ceramics were used to imitate the appearance of Portland stone or Carrara marble, and for the practical advantages of being washable and being lighter than stone. The London Underground stations designed by Leslie Green are some of the most vivid examples of Edwardian faience and show a unique degree of standardization. The same deep red colour and round-arched forms were used for the Northern, Bakerloo and Piccadilly lines.

By the 1920s, manufacturers found that chain-stores were probably their most important clients. Many of the Co-operative Societies had adopted white faience with Renaissance decoration as the basis of their house-style. The most prosperous terracotta firms of the inter-war period, such as Hathern of Loughborough, Leicestershire, or Shaw's of Darwen, Lancashire, gained numerous orders for such frontages.

Faience was accepted as the ideal material for fronting cinemas, being fireproof and, through colour and exotic styles, conveying the spirit of luxury and escapism which Rivolis, Coliseums or Odeons used to attract audiences to silent films and then the 'talkies'. Hathern gained a pre-eminence in supplying several of the chains through an almost unwavering tie with the greatest of cinema architects, George Coles. Three of Coles's designs dating to the end of the '20s present rich displays of polychromy: the Carltons in Upton Park (1928) and Islington (1930), were given façades in an Egyptian style with bulbous ribbed columns and coved cornices, while the Palace at Southall (1929) was Britain's only cinema in the Chinese style.

More streamlined images were adopted by Coles and Hathern for the Odeon cinemas of the late '30s. World War II virtually curtailed production of faience. Though demand revived in the '50s and '60s, shifts in architectural tastes and problems with fixing non-structural slabs and tiles deterred many architects from specifying architectural ceramics. Over the last decade Hathern and Shaw's have seen a renewed demand, both for incorporate sculptural decoration or bright colours. ❧

Select Bibliography

D Hamilton *Architectural Ceramics*, Thames & Hudson, London 1978
J Hawkins *The Poole Potteries*, Barrie & Jenkins, London 1980
M Stratton 'The Terracotta Industry: its Distribution, Manufacturing Processes and
    Products' *Industrial Archaeology Review*, VIII, No. 2, 1986

Pressing shop at Hathernware Ceramics, Loughborough, Leicestershire.

"...Germany, France and Belgium had followed the British lead..."

19TH AND EARLY-20TH CENTURY EUROPEAN TILES

Hans van Lemmen DIP ART ATC BA
SENIOR LECTURER IN ART AND
DESIGN HISTORY
LEEDS POLYTECHNIC

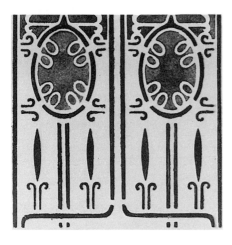

Dust-pressed tile with a stencilled, abstract Art Nouveau design made by the firm Rozenburg, The Hague, Holland, c.1900.

The continental scene during the 19th and early-20th century is complex and varied. On the one hand we have countries such as Holland, where the production of tiles remained within the tradition of hand-craft production, while on the other, Germany, France and Belgium had followed the British lead in terms of more mechanized tile production and decoration.

The invention of pressing dust-clay soon found its way to the Continent and according to Forrer, the firm Villeroy & Boch introduced the technique of dust-pressing for tile manufacture as early as 1846 in their factory at Septfontaines, Luxembourg. Germany soon became a formidable producer of tiles. Villeroy & Boch had factories in Germany at Mettlach, Dresden and Merzig in addition to Septfontaines. All were involved in tile production ranging from encaustic floor tiles to majolica tiles and mosaic.

In France a picture not unlike that of German tile production emerges. In Paris a number of prominent tile producers were active such as the firms Loebnitz et Fils and Bigot & Cie, while Muller & Cie were producing at Ivry-Port, near Paris. Boulenger was active at Auneuil, near Beauvais. This firm, under the direction of Jean-Baptiste Aimé Boulenger, specialized in encaustic tile production. Auneuil must be one of the most complete tile sites in France with its factory (no longer in production), its own Boulenger tile museum, and various outstanding tiled buildings in the town, all intact. Beauvais itself can boast a number of important 19th century tile producers such as the firm of Charles Gréber as well as the large encaustic tile factory of Colozier at Saint-Just-des Marais on the outskirts of the town. Unlike in Britain, in France encaustic tiles are just as frequently encountered on the wall as on the floor and their colour schemes are more adventurous. As well as the traditional brown, red and buff, at times we find grey, blue, white, pink and green predominating.

The manufacture of tin-glazed tiles was still carried on in France in the 19th century alongside the more mechanized industrial tile production. Many of these tiles were made in the area around Beauvais. Tin-glazed tiles were made at Ponchon and St Paul which show affinities with Dutch delftware and consist to a great extent of patterned tiles often executed with the aid of stencils rather than free-hand painting. The colours blue and purple predominate and they can be seen in old kitchens and fireplaces throughout France. The factory of Fourmaintraux at Devres in Pas-de-Calais made tin-glazed tiles and is still active today.

In Belgium there was the large firm of Boch Frères at La Louviere, established by Victor and Eugene Boch in 1844. They also operated a factory at Maubeuge just over the border in France which specialized in encaustic tiles and pavement quarries. Les Majoliques de Hasselt in Hasselt and Helman Céramique in Berchen St Agathe near Brussels made dust-pressed transfer-printed wall tiles.

In Holland throughout the 19th century tile production had been dominated by the manufacture of tin-glazed tiles which was essentially a hand process. Firms such as Tichelaar in Makkum, Tjallingi in Harlingen, and Ravesteijn and Schillemans in Utrecht were making traditional Dutch tiles with painted in-glaze decoration. In many ways they were continuing a tradition of tile manufacture established in Holland at the end of the 16th century. The mechanization of tile production took place on a small scale towards the end of the 19th century when a number of firms began to use the dust-pressing method. Rozenburg in The Hague, De Porcelyene Fles in Delft, Regout and Société Céramique in Maastricht were using tile presses to increase production. These dust-pressed tiles were decorated by the stencil technique and was done by Rozenburg and De Porcelyene Fles. Transfer printing was employed by Regout and Société Céramique, but dust-pressed tiles were also still painted by hand as can be seen from the panels produced by the firm Distel. ❧

Art Nouveau tile panel with a figure painted on dust-pressed tiles by the Dutch firm Distel, c.1905. (In situ in the porch of 168 Ferdinand Bolstraat, Amsterdam.)

Select Bibliography

R Forrer *Geschichte der europaischen Fliesen-Keramik*, Strasburg 1901
M Weisser *Jugenstil Fliesen* Verlag Dieter Fricke, Frankfurt 1983

PICTURE-TILES IN THE 20TH CENTURY

Chris Blanchett
NEWSLETTER EDITOR
TILES & ARCHITECTURAL CERAMICS
SOCIETY

Carter, Stabler & Adams hand-painted tile of a Dutch seaman from the 'Blue Dutch' series, c.1920. Designed by Joseph Roelants. (Private collection.)

Following the boom in tile production and the proliferation of smaller manufacturers during the closing years of the 19th century, the early part of the 20th century was a period of consolidation and take-over during which tile production decreased significantly. By the beginning of World War I, tile production had slumped to less than a fifth of the 1900 figure and the war itself brought a further reduction due to wartime economies.

In the early 1920s, Art Nouveau began to give way to Art Deco but the new angular, strident forms did not lend themselves to the design of individual tiles. Occasionally there were attempts to use tiling in architectural schemes but these usually achieved their effect by use of shaped tiles and colour, rather than individually designed tiles. Perhaps as a reaction to this there was a resurgence of interest in hand-decoration, usually in the form of tube-lining or in-glaze painting. The designs, however, were far removed from their Victorian counterparts, being intended to stand as individual decorative devices, often set in a field of plain tiling. This was most apparent in fireplace design; where the Victorians had used tiles to give a splash of colour to a black cast-iron frame, now tiles were used to create whole fireplaces, utilizing strong geometric form enhanced by the eggshell glazes developed in the 1920s. This strongly geometric form was softened, or perhaps accentuated, by the inclusion of a few hand-decorated tiles.

Probably the most successful and influential pottery producing company in the 1920s was that of Carter, Stabler & Adams. It was established in 1921 at Poole, Dorset, as a subsidiary of Carter & Co, itself the successor to the Architectural Pottery Co and a successful manufacturer of tiles in the late-19th and early-20th centuries. They specialized in producing hand-painted tiles which had much in common with their ranges of art pottery. The tiles were painted in-glaze, as delftware tiles had been before them, utilizing a matt tin-glaze, applied to a pressed plastic-clay body which caused the glaze to craze in a characteristic fashion.

One of the earliest series of tiles to come from Carter's, possibly before the formation of Carter, Stabler & Adams, was the *Coloured Dutch* series designed by Belgian refugee Joseph Roelants in about 1918–20. This series, which was also produced in monochrome blue (*Blue Dutch* series), depicted traditional Dutch scenes drawn in great detail, yet full of life. The designs were framed by a single line and were unlike delftware tiles in style and composition. The popularity of these tiles was illustrated by the fact that they were still being produced (by silk-screening) in the late 1950s. Roelants was also responsible for a series of *Blue Boats* (and possibly *Coloured Boats*) depicting Dutch sailing boats in similar format to the *Blue Dutch* series.

To cater for younger tastes, Carter produced several children's series of tiles including *Nursery Rhymes* and *Nursery Toys* by Dora Batty (*c*.1922) and *Playbox* by A B Read. Utilizing the strong colours which had been developed for their Art Deco pottery ranges, these tiles were quite striking and looked superb when set among plain tiles in a nursery fireplace. The *Farmyard* series designed by E E Stickland (*c*.1925) is probably best known in its four-tile panel version, produced up to the 1960s for Dewhurst butcher's shops. Both the 5in and 6in single tiles and the four-tile panels were unusual in being stencilled and then outlined by hand.

Carter also produced a number of flower series including two by Reginald Till and a very Art Deco set by Truda Carter. In a rather different vein, the *Chase* and *Sporting* sets by Eric Bawden, from the early 1930s, were clever little humorous caricatures, while the *Waterbirds* series by Harold Stabler captured the life and movement of its subjects with a few simple brush strokes. Stabler also designed a series of moulded tiles for the London Underground in 1938–9, examples of which can still be seen at some of central London's older stations, although they are rapidly disappearing in programmes of refurbishment.

Carter also used independent designers and a particular example of this is the *Dogs* series designed by Cecil Aldin, well known for his comic paintings of dogs. This series is unusual in that the designer's signature appears on the tiles. Carter continued to produce picture tiles well into the 1960s until their amalgamation with Pilkington's Tiles Ltd in 1964, and were pioneers in the art of silk-screen printing, producing both new ranges and re-workings of older designs.

Packard & Ord hand-painted tile depicting a ship in a circle from the 'Fair Life' series, c.1930. Designed and painted by Sylvia Packard using a Carter blank. (Private collection.)

Although perhaps better know for their late-Victorian and Art Nouveau designs, including many by Lewis F Day, Pilkington also produced a number of picture-tiles during the '20s and '30s. Unlike Carter most of Pilkington's picture tiles were tube-lined and often tended to be smaller, mostly 4in square. Whilst many of the themes were similar, there is a marked contrast in style between the two companies' products, the Pilkington designs generally filling the tile completely and sometimes containing elements which linked adjacent tiles together enabling them to form a frieze or dado. This is illustrated by their series of *Sailing Ships* or *Fish* where not only the waves provide continuity, but also a dotted border at the top and bottom of each tile. The colours used on these tiles were extremely strong and brilliant and they looked superb against a background of plain tiles. The *Old Time Ships* series was also produced in larger format over 12 or 24 tiles, when a chequered border was introduced to frame the composition. The design of these tiles is generally attributed to Edmund Kent who was also responsible for their decoration.

Not to be outdone by Carter, Pilkington also featured a series of *Farmyard Animals* (hand-painted) and a *Nursery Rhyme* set produced on 9in x 6in tiles designed by Margaret Pilkington. These are particularly effective, using a very wide palette of colours, but are extremely rare today and were too expensive to be widely used. Pilkington's foray into picture tiles was comparatively short-lived and by about 1935 production had virtually ceased.

Not all 1920s and '30s picture-tiles were made by the large companies; there were a number of smaller organizations which did decorating only. The most significant of these was Packard & Ord, a company which is still in business today, trading as Marlborough Ceramic Tiles, Marlborough, Wiltshire. Sylvia Packard and Rosalind Ord, the founders, were art teachers at the Royal School, Bath, and their introduction to tile decorating came in 1929 when they designed and painted a tile mural for the school to line one wall of a corridor from the main building to the gymnasium. Rosalind Ord became fascinated by the craft and undertook a three week course at the Central School of Art, London, to learn *'all about glazes'*! Following a number of small commissions the two women developed a number of standard series of tile designs, some of which are still in production today. The biscuit tiles they used were bought from Carter's, Poole, and after decoration were returned there for firing. In 1936 Miss Packard moved from Bath to Hungerford, nearer to the Ord family home in Marlborough and the two women bought a former builder's yard for £250 and installed their first kiln. They were soon joined by Thea

Packard & Ord hand-painted tile of a woodcutter from the 'Peasants' series, c.1930. Designed and painted by Rosalind Ord using a Carter blank. (Private collection.)

Bridges who designed at least three sets of tiles including the wonderfully idiosyncratic *Sporting Set* series. Soon the little company counted even Fortnum & Mason among its clients, but before the business really took off World War II intervened and the kilns were let to a Dutchman for charcoal making (which ruined them).

In 1945, when the war was over, Rosalind Ord wanted to restart the business but Sylvia Packard felt the time had come to retire, so Hugh Robb, a near-neighbour of Miss Ord, bought her share and set the venture on a firm commercial basis. Because of post-war austerity it was difficult to sell tiles as such, so they sought to market the tiles made into trays, tables and even wall lights. Biscuit tiles were bought from H & G Thynne, Pilkington, Rhodes and others, and soon as many as 30 paintresses were employed. In 1951–52 over 12,000 trays were made and sold, including many made as souvenirs of the 1953 coronation. The company anticipated the boom in fireplace manufacture and opened its own workshops to make the then fashionable slabbed fireplaces using marble and slate as well as tiles.

Whilst many of Packard & Ord's tile series were floral designs, they also produced a number of literary sets including the *Shakespeare* and *Dickens* sets and a *Nursery Rhymes* series that owed a lot to the earlier Carter's series by Dora Batty. Also featured in their catalogues were series of *Song Birds, Game Birds* and *Cock and Hens* and the country influence was also present in Sylvia Packard's *Pastoral* and *English Country Life* series. Contemporary kitchen and bathroom design was also catered for by the *Kitchen Things* and *Yachts* series, among others. By the late 1950s, however, the market for hand-painted tiles was declining and the company turned to screen-printed designs to maintain its market. This side of the business is today the most significant but in recent years the company has started production of its own terracotta body which is again being decorated by hand, often to the original Packard & Ord designs.

A lesser-known contemporary of Packard & Ord was the firm of Dunsmore Tiles, probably founded in the late '20s by the Misses Brace and Fisher, who were, by the early '50s, operating from an address in Campden Hill, London. Two techniques appear to have been used by the company: hand-painting, which seems to have been done freehand and with the aid of stencils; and aerograph and stencil. This latter seems to be the main method used and was applied to series of *Farmyard Scenes, Birds, Animals* and a wonderful *Alice in Wonderland* series by C F A Voysey, based on the original Tenniel illustrations.

Dunsmore Tiles was, however, best known for its *Fish* series which was stencilled and then outlined by hand, much as Carter's *Farmyard* series

Carter, Stabler & Adams stencilled tile of a turkey from the 'Farmyard' series, c.1925. Designed by E E Strickland using a Carter blank. (Private collection.)

had been. A distinctive feature of these tiles was that after painting the artist wiped across the surface of the tiles removing some of the colour. When glazed this gave a real impression of the fish 'swimming' in the glaze. Incidentally, many Dunsmore tiles have been wrongly attributed to Minton, whose blanks they used (not exclusively) as the only marking employed was a small rubber-stamped 'DUNSMORE TILES', which easily washes off. It is to be hoped that much more will be learnt regarding this interesting company, particularly with regard to the decorative techniques used. Dunsmore Tiles eventually went out of business in the mid-1950s.

As times change so do tastes and regrettably the market for picture tiles has dwindled, but there is an exciting trend among modern-day craft potters to design and produce hand-decorated tiles which in some respects are the successors to these earlier tiles. If they give as much pleasure as their predecessors they will have succeeded in their primary aim – the fusion of education, art and architecture. ❧

Dunsmore aerographed and stencilled tile of a lamb from the 'Farm Animals' series, c.1930. Designer unknown. Minton blank. (Private collection.)

Select Bibliography

A J Cross *Pilkington's Royal Lancastrian Pottery and Tiles*, Richard Dennis
    Publications, London 1980
Dunsmore Tiles 'Broadsheet', ND *c*.1950
J Hawkins *The Poole Potteries*, Barrie & Jenkins, London 1980
S Rasey *A Brief History of Marlborough Tiles and Tile Products 1936–1986*,
    Packard & Ord, Marlborough 1987

Catalogues
Packard & Ord trade catalogues, 1950, 1951, 1956, ND *c*.1962

"...uniting art and architecture by the use of ceramic tiles..."

AVANT-GARDE ARTISTS AND TILES

The 20th century has seen a succession of movements and innovations in the arts. It has been a century of constant change and experimentation, a restless search for style. Although these movements originated in Europe, in this century architecture and the fine and decorative arts have become international. At the beginning of the century many seminal artists were using multi-media to express visual ideas and some painters, when commissioned to produce work for buildings, used the age-old solution of uniting art and architecture by the use of ceramic tiles.

Henri Matisse (1869–1954)

Matisse was an artist who moved from Impressionism into a style of painting known as Fauvism (from the French *fauves* meaning 'wild beasts'). His work was concerned with line, colour, space and design. He was a master at organizing these elements on a two-dimensional surface. A major commission came his way in 1947, towards the end of his life, when he was asked to provide designs for the chapel of Notre-Dame du Rosaire at Vence in southern France. Apart from the stained glass windows, Matisse undertook work for three major and two minor tiled ceramic mural paintings consisting of black-line drawings on a white ground. The bleak economic starkness of the panels is arresting. Matisse drew the final designs on full size cartoons divided into squares the exact size of the tiles. Unglazed tiles were brought from the kilns of the ceramicist Boudillon at Aubagne, near Marseilles, and laid on the artist's floor. Matisse drew the heavy black lines with a brush directly on to the tiles which were then returned for glazing and firing. The three large panels represent the *Virgin*

Josie Montgomery
CURATOR OF ART
SCARBOROUGH ART GALLERY

Ceramic mural in the chapel of Notre-Dame du Rosaire, painted by Matisse, depicting the 'Virgin and Child'. Designed and executed between 1947–51.

and Child, *St Dominic*, and one panel with the 14 *Stations of the Cross* in a single composition. What characterizes these tile panels is a spiritual presence without bulk, colour texture or detailed features. Their transparency enhanced by the lines of the tiles become images of weightlessness and pure luminosity.

Joan Miró (1893–1983)

Joan Miró is an internationally known Spanish painter who was born in Barcelona and studied ceramics there as a student. His paintings are fanciful, peopled by strange symbolic shapes and creatures. He went to Paris and became influenced by Surrealism. His later work suggests infinite and celestial space inhabited by Bosch-like creatures from another world, painted in clear bright colours with childlike simplicity. The designs are fluid and curvilinear. The shapes have their own vigour and life, like amoebae evolving – they are not abstractions. Sometimes his work is whimsical but other themes are basic and serious, like the universal creative process of motherhood, or the horror of universal destructiveness.

Miró rediscovered ceramics in 1949–50 when it became not just a medium or technique but a means to the truth – a return to the earth and tradition. In 1957–8, he was commissioned to work on the UNESCO building in Paris and created *The Wall of the Sun* (1958) and *The Wall of the Moon* (1960). These tiled panels, and also another panel for Harvard University in 1961, reflect the beauty of Romanesque walls mixed with the primitive fantasy of cave paintings, both interpreted poetically and with a sense of reverence. The tiles each bear a fragment of the whole but also remain beautiful tiles in themselves. The walls are reminiscent of the coloured walls of Babylon but with new, free and fantastic poetic rhythms and motifs.

Antonio Gaudí (1852–1926)

This Spanish architect has been responsible for some of the most memorable structural images in the history of architecture. He is unique among 20th century designers, fusing his own personal Spanishness with incredible organic forms. Gothic and Art Nouveau elements have a strong Moorish influence, but he himself said he was simply continuing the Gothic tradition in Spain. Out of this rich mixture has come a once-and-for-all personal style. The structures of his buildings seem to writhe and move about as if they are living organisms at the mercy of restless elements. Gaudí has been claimed by the Surrealists and many 20th century movements but although his influence is there, his work stands alone in its absolute individuality.

Gaudí's benches decorated with broken tiles in the Park Güell, Barcelona, 1900–14.

As luck would have it, Gaudí's first major work was a suburban villa commissioned by Vicens, a ceramic and tile manufacturer from Barcelona. The Vicens House, 1883–85, has a richly fretted façade of rubble stone and pink brick girdled with floral ceramic tiles. Inside, this richness is continued especially in a small smoking room which is lined with ceramic and heavily embossed papier-mâché tiles. While this house was being built, Gaudí was planning *El Capricho* in Comillas, northern Spain. The main block has a rusticated stone base above which the yellow brick work is banded with 6 in square tiles embossed with yellow and brown sunflowers. These together with plain green lustre tiles cover the tower and frame the windows. The building glows in a Moorish style.

Gaudí's patronage came from the up-and-coming industrialists whose wealth came from the textile industry. Count Eusebio Güell, one of these industrialists, had inherited a fortune from his father's spinning mills and apart from his textile interests, established a Portland cement company, a great help to Gaudí. Güell's partnership with Gaudí began in 1884 with the construction of two pavilions for Güell's estate on the outskirts of Barcelona. These two single-storied buildings, connected by a brilliant iron dragon gateway, are a concentration of Gaudí's rich combination of materials – pink and yellow brickwork set off by the sparkle of fragments of ceramic embedded in the mortar-pressed stucco decoration, stone rubble coloured tiles and a variety of wrought, cast- and meshed-iron. The buildings look Moorish in style and reflect the fashionable interest in Arabic art. The later Güell Palace of 1885–90 looks more like a Spanish stronghold, but inside is a magical dome of deep blue tiles sparkling with stars. On the roof Gaudí introduced his first play space, chimney pots and ventilation shafts covered in multi coloured broken ceramic tiles.

The Park Güell, 1900–14, was originally intended as a garden suburb on a hill on the outskirts of Barcelona but was finally converted into a municipal park and is the finest example of Gaudí's sensitive collaboration with nature. A boundary wall is decorated with circular ceramic nameplates. The main entrance is flanked by two gatekeepers' buildings which have elaborate ceramic-coated roofs. A double flight of stairs with ceramic banisters have, in the centre, a ceramic dragon or lizard – a sculpture covered in broken pieces of tile. The inward leaning Doric columns of the recessed market hall have white ceramic leggings. Broken ceramic and glass mosaics cover the cupped domes of the roof. The open arena and terrace above the market hall is edged with a snaking ceramic bench. All kinds of tiles and broken tiles coat the warped surfaces of this happy idea. The extraordinary creative use of tiles in and on his buildings has set Gaudí apart as one of the great masters of decorative architectural design at the turn of the century.

De Stijl Artists in Holland: Theo van Doesburg and Bart van der Leck

The De Stijl movement in Holland, 1917–31, was an important development in the history of 20th century art and design. These artists formulated an abstract language in painting which influenced furniture, interior design and architecture. Among them were Mondrian, Van Doesburg, Van der Leck and Rietveld. They voiced their ideas in a magazine also called *De Stijl*. This new aesthetic manifested itself through severe abstraction into the straight line, the square and rectangular forms which were easily adapted to the use of tiles in architecture.

In 1917, Theo van Doesburg became leader of the Dutch avant-garde group, De Stijl. In that year the architect, J P Oud, was commissioned to design a holiday home for factory girls from Leyden. The house, De Vonk, was built in 1918–19 at Noordwijkerhout on the Dutch coast. Most of the exterior and interior decoration was left to Van Doesburg who designed glazed brick panels for the outside entrance and tiled floors for the entrance hall and landing. The central doorway has a large horizontal glazed brick panel above the entrance with two smaller panels on either side below the windows. The glazed bricks are yellow, blue, green, white and black, forming horizontal and vertical rectangles with the cement spacing acting as a grid between each colour area. Inside the building the tiled floors have patterns of black, white and buff square tiles making up patterns which are repeated in complex ways and interact with other features.

Bart van der Leck also produced a large ceramic mural for VARA Broadcasting Studio in Hilversum, just before his death in 1958. This mural comes very close to his painting, *Horseman*, of 1918. The images were built up of geometrical units in red, blue and yellow on a white ground and represented symbols associated with the broadcasting company. The panel, consisting of 682 tiles, was made by the firm Porceleyne Fles in Delft and was fixed on the exterior of the building in 1961.

Salvador Dali (1904–89)

Salvador Dali was the most notorious of the Surrealists whose paranoid dream images were painted with meticulous truth. Time, form and space were distorted in a frighteningly real way. In 1950, Maurice Duchin of New York commissioned Dali to design a set of six tiles for decorative use on internal or external walls or for sun patios and balconies. The Dali-designed tiles were produced and hand-painted in 1954 by El Siglio, a well known

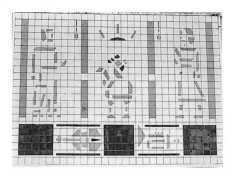

Tile panel designed by Bart van der Leck and executed by the firm Porceleyne Fles for the VARA Broadcasting Studio, Hilversum, Holland, 1961.

tile manufacturing company in Valencia, Spain. Duchin also licensed El Siglio to reproduce a limited edition of the tiles for sale in Europe, possibly some 4,000 sets. The tiles represented three pairs of basic themes, *War and Peace, Love and Music* and *Life and Death*. Dali managed to give unique visual expression to these elemental themes common to all people. *Death* is symbolized by the image of a dead starfish on the beach, while *War* is represented as four aggressive arrows closing in on the centre of the tile. Each tile shows Dali's signature.

Pablo Picasso (1881–1973)

This multi-faceted artist lived throughout the revolutionary changes in art at the end of the 19th and beginning of the 20th centuries, progressing through many styles and helping to create one himself – Cubism. His restless creativity covered painting, sculpture, print-making and ceramics. He began to decorate ceramics in 1946 when he met Georges Ramié who ran a pottery with his wife, Suzanne, in Vallauris, southern France. Picasso decorated ready-made wares such as plates, vases and dishes and also made his own unique pottery very much akin to his paintings. He also decorated tile blanks. His tiles and plaques bear faces, scenes from Spanish bullfights and erotic scenes. Most of them were done during the second half of the 1950s and throughout the 1960s. The techniques employed varied considerably – some tiles were painted, others had incised lines in combination with painted colours. There were also several simple, unglazed, orange-red terracotta plaques with incised decorations only. A selection of his tiles can be seen at the Musée Picasso, Paris.

Bernard Leach (1887–1979)

Bernard Leach began his career as a fine artist but later chose a craft, ceramics, to express his individual creativity. He later subdued his natural romanticism deeming it feeble indulgence, but his own personal vision is always clearly to be seen even when his forms are at their most Classical. He started with a small workshop founded on a core of repetitive pottery but he always kept a place for creative, unique, pieces. He remained a hand-craftsman in an industrial society. He thought in primal images, putting plain and simple work on an elevated plane. He had a tremendous influence on potters and pottery in Britain and, as he himself had been influenced by living in Japan and by studying Chinese art of the Sung Dynasty, so the eastern traditions became the base of British craft pottery.

Leach believed pottery was a noble, ancient art the world over and that there should be one world and one art message. He had made his

Ceramic plaque decorated by Picasso in 1962.

home in St Ives, Cornwall, and a number of the tiles he made had Cornish images. They were stoneware tiles, made from the late 1920s through the 1940s, with mottled buff glazes, on brown, blue or cream grounds. Some had animal and landscape subjects. The Leach family have continued in ceramic work and have also made tiles, carrying on the tradition with their own distinct individual images.

John Piper (b. 1903)

John Piper was born in Surrey and studied painting at the Royal College of Art and the Slade School of Art. He is a landscape painter who creates an 'English' atmosphere in his work. The paintings often have architectural subjects and some are abstractions. The 'lesser' arts have taken a major place in Piper's working life. He has always had a close relation with the decorative arts, bringing his fine art skills of painting, drawing and colour into stained glass, textiles and ceramics. He has often worked with craftsmen, and in the case of ceramics, with Geoffrey Eastop. The decorations on his tiles are mostly heads or decorative abstract designs. Another group made in association with the Fulham Pottery, London, include landscape variations after the Old Masters. His playful mood of decoration recalls at times English slipware, Renaissance majolica or Picasso's painted ceramics. A special set of four screen-printed tiles designed by John Piper, representing the seasons, was made in 1983 for the John Piper exhibition at the Tate Gallery, London. ❧

Select Bibliography

A H Barr *Matisse: His Art and His Public*, Secker & Warburg, London 1975
C Hogben *Art of Bernard Leach*, Faber & Faber, London 1978
G Ramié *Ceramique de Picasso*, Editions Albin Michel, Paris 1984

"...by the 1980s decorative tiles were really back in full swing..."

CONTEMPORARY TILE ARTISTS

The latter years of the 1970s marked an optimistic turning point for the future of tiles in Britain. World War I caused the depletion of work-forces at many of the major tile-making companies and the subsequent demand for decorative tiles was in any case considerably reduced as plain surfaces became the preferred modern style. The decades up to the 1970s largely produced a decorative desert of plain and mottled mass-produced tiles. They were relieved only by the occasional oasis of colour and pattern from small-scale decorators such as Sylvia Packard and Rosalind Ord or the designer-inspired products from a few larger companies such as Carter & Co of Poole, Dorset. These represent the continuous thread of creative tile decoration which links the Arts and Crafts Movement of the 1890s with the present day.

The decorative tile renaissance began to show signs of real life in the mid-1970s with craftspeople such as Maggie Angus Berkowitz and Jean Powell producing highly colourful, one-off 'works of art' on tiles to be used as murals, often in public places. Work such as this was nearly always done to commission either from an individual client or possibly through an enlightened interior designer or architect. Few 'designer' tiles were being speculatively produced, it being almost unheard of for a small hand-producing firm to offer a 'range' of decorative tiles that could be mixed and matched or added to *ad infinitum*.

By the 1980s decorative tiles were really back in full swing. It was almost a revival of the 1880s, though this time around the drive and energy producing the lively new designs was coming not from within the remaining established tile firms, but from individuals or small companies

Kathryn Huggins
MEMBERSHIP SECRETARY
TILES & ARCHITECTURAL CERAMICS
SOCIETY

Tube-lined, hand-painted owl panel by Kenneth Clark Ceramics, Lewes, Sussex.

71

anxious to express their art on uniform slabs of clay. Coupled with this, a renewed awareness and desire for colour and decoration in buildings provided just the right climate for craftspeople to respond with creativity and entrepreneurial flair. Small-scale operations have the additional bonus of flexibility which has, to some extent, resulted in a client-led market. Many of the most exciting schemes and projects produced today are the imaginative interpretations of clients' ideas manifested by the artist, the tile decorator, through the medium of ceramic glaze colours.

One of the oldest firms still decorating tiles is Kenneth Clark Ceramics, Lewes, Sussex. This family firm, with over 35 years of experience, has built up an enviable range of designs. Kenneth Clark has concentrated on developing their impressive, subtle glaze colours while his wife, Ann, has worked on the designs. Spanning so many years and many changes in fashion the Clarks' tiles amply demonstrate the flexibility of workshop scale production.

Paul Henry, of London, who under his own name designs and paints some very exciting tiles and as Purbeck Decorative Tile Co produces mainly silk-screened designs as standard lines, has recently completed a delightfully whimsical nursery bathroom scheme. As an artist with a very broad palette, he is able to produce designs to suit almost every situation which can, and often do, include an element of fun. His designs are certainly distinctive and yet sufficiently different from each other to make attribution difficult.

Some people bring a more strikingly cohesive feel to their work. Gathering her training in the UK, Italy, Africa and the USA, Maggie Angus Berkowitz has had a deep well of experience to draw from. She has been painting on tiles for many years and is one of Britain's leading tile mural painters. Her work exhibits a strength and boldness through her skilful, confident use of line and colour. Her work consists mainly of 'pictures' for walls, floors and worktops and one of her specialities has been devising permanent, large-scale 'board games' on ceramic floor tiles and, as a logical sequence to that, she has recently completed a tile 'labyrinth' in the foyer of a company headquarters in Royston, Hertfordshire.

Working in Portsmouth, Jan O'Highway's designs show the same kind of exuberance and vigour through flamboyant use of colour. Many of her designs are derived from a naturalistic base but are then pulled and abstracted into really exotic affairs. Jan is first and foremost a painter and considers her formal art training in figurative work an extremely valuable asset.

Not all tile decorators have the advantage of Bronwyn Williams-Ellis's artistic pedigree. Based in Bath, her designs, mostly naturalistic and

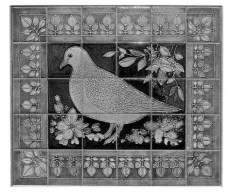

Tube-lined, hand-painted pigeon panel by Kenneth Clark Ceramics, Lewes, Sussex.

jauntily arranged, exhibit a delightful spontaneity and freshness. Like Gesine Mahoney, of Newquay, Cornwall, and Frances Beresford, of Barton-on-Humber, Humberside, both of whose work is executed in a very 'painterly' manner and frequently using naturalistic subjects, Bronwyn Williams-Ellis has found that the rekindled appeal of an Aga cooker at the heart of the family kitchen has provided an excellent tabloid for finely decorated tiles – practical, pretty and, like the Aga, long-lasting. Clients are prepared to spend considerable sums of money having something very special designed and painted on that panel.

Most of the people so far mentioned decorate tiles using an on-glaze method of painting and are, it should be said, reliant upon the big commercial tile manufacturers for the supply of their blanks. There is nothing new or very unusual in this; it is well known that William De Morgan purchased blank tiles from Craven Dunnill at Jackfield, Shropshire. Coincidentally Su Turner, who now operates her tile decorating workshop in part of the old Craven Dunnill factory, is captivated by the work of William De Morgan and is able to produce designs which capture his style. Other more unusual historical sources for her tiles include illuminated manuscripts, which she embellishes in the medieval style with glaze containing ground gold.

Victorian tile designs have provided a great stimulus for many of the new wave of tile decorators, but Bobby Jones has taken his brief from a century earlier. He specializes in the under-glaze painting techniques associated with 18th century tin-glaze. His work is scholarly and authentic, utilizing 5in-square tiles and tin-opacified glazes – but that is not to say dull; apart from his blue-and-white tiles a range of more immediately modern designs are produced exploiting the same tin-glaze techniques. Bobby Jones has found much of the inspiration for his new designs in the Shropshire countryside around his home and workshop.

Stephen Cocker, of Bedale, Yorkshire, whose *Cosmos* tiles, interpreting the elements, are as bright, fresh and timeless as a spring day, has also found enormous inspiration in the everyday world about him. Unencumbered by formal training, he is a natural artist. He has used his background as gamekeeper for the Duke of Marlborough to develop his eye for nature. Many of his designs take nature as their starting point but are then keenly and boldly treated to a dose of whimsicality. This treatment adds to their appeal enormously and also serves to make his designs geographically anonymous.

Clearly the vast majority of small-scale tile decoration being carried out at the present time involves individuals painting directly onto

Printed and hand-decorated tiles in the 'Woodland' series by Kenneth Clark Ceramics, Lewes, Sussex.

commercially produced blanks. The fruits of their labours are almost always intended to be seen in a vertical format, be it behind the Aga or beside the swimming pool. However, the overwhelming number of skilled people in this field should not obstruct our view of some very important and lively work in the area of floor tiles. Diana Hall, whose workshop is at Iford, Sussex, has been making medieval-style encaustic floor tiles for several years. She also produces printed floor tiles working closely with Peggy Angus, the octogenarian wallpaper and tile designer. Diana Hall's tiles have been used in locations ranging from conservation work in Ely Cathedral to new public art at Milton Keynes, Buckinghamshire.

Falling firmly into the traditional craft camp are Rupert Spira and Judith Rowe who together run Froyle Tiles, near Alton, Hampshire. Rupert Spira was apprenticed to the famous studio potter Michael Cardew and now, unusually, specializes in floor tiles made of stoneware clay. Glazes on these tiles, largely due to the very high temperatures (1,300°C) which stoneware is subjected to have a great richness and subtlety of colour quite unlike any glaze found on an earthenware body.

One further company promoting the return of decorative tiles is the aptly named Life Enhancing Tile Co. This young Portsmouth firm has taken its design remit from all over the world. This eclecticism has resulted in a series of startlingly fresh encaustic tiles bearing unfamiliar motifs that look as if they might have come direct from Mexico or Peru.

The economic climate of the 1980s provided a particularly stimulating environment for small businesses. It was a period of extremes; a time which saw quantum leaps in home ownership and perhaps more importantly in home awareness and beautification. We were all 'designer' conscious and the individual 'different' idea or scheme for products from tiles to telephones won hands down. At the same time the government was encouraging people to become self-employed in order to mitigate colossal unemployment figures. Attractive incentives such as the Enterprise Allowance Scheme were introduced. In this arena of free enterprise many individuals, who might not otherwise have taken the plunge, flourished. The Prince of Wales added his support to this enterprise in the form of the Prince's Youth Business Trust and several tile people, including The Decorative Tile Works and Su Turner, both of whom operate from Jackfield, Shropshire, have benefited from it.

The recent renaissance of decorative tiles, cursorily recorded here with many omissions, points to the need for a major exhibition and scholarly catalogue all of its own. Let up hope that not too many years elapse before this comes to fruition. ❧

"...tiles and architectural ceramics will have a continuing history..."

THE SOCIETY'S FIRST TEN YEARS

In July 1980 I received a letter from Hans van Lemmen which included the prophetic words, *'I think the time has come (and other collectors are thinking likewise) to set up a British Tile Society. If placed on a proper footing it could make a valuable contribution to the knowledge and study of tiles'*. Richard Myers of Bath had already started a tile newsletter and the groundswell of interest in tiles at the end of the 1970s amply demonstrated Victor Hugo's belief that an invasion of armies can be resisted but not an idea whose time has come.

The first step towards a Society was a conjugation of like minds in February 1981, held appropriately enough in an upper room at the Barton Arms, one of Birmingham's best tiled pubs. Here the embryo Tiles & Architectural Ceramics Society was conceived and its 'parents' began preparations for a short and highly planned pregnancy.

The birth of the Society took place at 7.00pm on 4 April 1981 and had been carefully engineered to coincide with a weekend conference on architectural ceramics organized by Michael Stratton of the Institute of Industrial Archaeology at the Ironbridge Gorge Museum, Shropshire. This at least ensured that about 50 people could be signed up for membership within the Society's first 24 hours of life! After a witty toast from Francis Celoria, the then Director of the Gladstone Pottery Museum, Stoke-on-Trent (who became the Society's first Chairman), and a rousing refrain from the Jackfield Silver Band, the Society began life in earnest. In its early months a constitution was hammered out and charitable status sought from the Charity Commissioners – both unglamorous but vital developments being piloted by the new Society's Treasurer, John Greene.

Tony Herbert BSC DIP CONS
CHAIRMAN
TILES & ARCHITECTURAL CERAMICS
SOCIETY

Membership of the Society has come from a remarkably diverse background representing tile collectors, museum curators, ceramic crafts people and conservators, designers and architects. A conscious policy to avoid a London bias for both committee and general meetings has helped the geographical spread of membership and a constant feature has been the ten per cent of members from outside Britain, notably from the USA but including countries as distant as Japan and Brazil.

The real value of the work of voluntary societies in Britain comes through their publications, which act as a vital forum for scholarship in specialist fields. Never was this truer than in the 1980s when the fashion for 'market forces' frequently displaced academic scholarship from the work of institutions such as museums. The Society's original intention was to publish a quarterly bulletin and an annual journal. The latter proved over-optimistic and the *Journal* has become what librarians conveniently refer to as an 'occasional' publication with three volumes appearing in ten years. The bulletin came out under the title *Glazed Expressions*, whose hint of humour has helped to dispel the sanctimonious image which bedevils some specialist societies. In its distinctive maroon livery, members have received 22 issues during the decade providing over 230 pages and a formidable corpus of original material, complete with index.

The unravelling of the fascinating story of Medmenham tiles and the growing body of information on back-marks are just two of the areas in which *Glazed Expressions* has played a vital publishing role in recording material of lasting value. The quarterly *Newsletter* emerged in 1985 when the need for a medium of communication with members became apparent which would allow for news items and other snippets of interesting but often ephemeral information.

The other popular and more sociable aspect of the Society's work has been the organization of visits and events of which there have been over 50 including a few European visits. There is something particularly satisfying about pursuing an interest in the company of like-minded people. But gazing as a gaggle at glazed ceramics once brought Society members close to arrest in busy Birmingham until a bemused pair of policemen were reassured that the tiles might be crazed but we were not crazy! On another memorable occasion the small group of members who clambered up long ladders to the scaffold around the Royal Albert Hall, London, are unlikely to forget either the close view of the splendid ceramic frieze or vertiginous glimpses of the axial formality of the main buildings of 'Albertopolis'.

The Society has supported the abolition of sex discrimination in novel ways such as arranging for mixed groups to view the magnificent tiled gents' lavatories beneath King William's statue, Hull, and those in the Philharmonic Hotel, Liverpool. The willing co-operation of owners and occupiers of important tiled buildings has been very gratifying and in some instances the Society has been able to return a favour by supplying more detailed historical information, as happened after the visit to the Palace of Holyroodhouse, Edinburgh, where an identification of Dutch delftware tiles was made.

The Society included the protection of tiles and architectural ceramics in its original objectives but in the ten years of its existence conservation has become an increasingly important issue. Decisions on what needs to be preserved should be based on facts, not fancy. To this end, research by Society members, and in particular the Location Index of tiles and architectural ceramics has been valuable. John Greene's survey of tile panels in hospitals, *Brightening the Long Days,* published under the Society's name in 1987, is an example of what can be achieved by dedicated individuals. Local authorities, private architects and individual owners of tiles have increasingly approached the Society for help and advice on the cleaning, restoration, relocation and replacement of tiles and to provide a basis for this a set of guidelines was produced and printed as a supplement to *Glazed Expressions* 16 in 1988.

The Society has benefited enormously from those of its members involved in the contemporary manufacture and decoration of tiles. Works visits have been very popular taking in the large-scale architectural ceramics of Hathern of Loughborough, Leicestershire, and Shaws of Darwen, Lancashire, the mass-production of H & R Johnsons, Stoke-on-Trent, Dennis Ruabon, North Wales and Carter's of Poole (Pilkington's) as well as the smaller craft-based production of individuals. This healthy pre-occupation with the present helps to ensure that the use of tiles and architectural ceramics will have a continuing history. ❧

The Minton, Hollins & Co factory building in Stoke-on-Trent was designed by Charles Lynam and built in 1869. In 1988 its proposed demolition became the subject of a public inquiry which was the first at which the Tiles & Architectural Ceramics Society was represented, demonstrating its growing role in the sphere of conservation.

GLOSSARY

ART DECO: Name for the decorative arts of the 1920s and '30s, often recognized by its use of severely stylized, streamlined or geometrical forms. Derived from the French term *arts décoratifs*.

ART NOUVEAU: A new form of decorative art at the end of the 19th and beginning of the 20th centuries characterized by its use of sensuous and sinuous lines. An expressive name first given to it was the 'whiplash style'.

ARTS AND CRAFTS MOVEMENT: A movement of British designers and architects (Morris, Voysey, Webb, etc.) who, during the second half of the 19th century, changed the nature of Victorian design by making it more true to the surface for which it was intended. Work done by hand, flat design and simplification of natural form are the hallmarks of this movement. It had a marked influence on tiles.

ART TILE: A name used during the second half of the 19th century for tiles showing the influence of contemporary design movements, such as the Arts and Crafts Movement and Art Nouveau, and which often have a special aesthetic quality.

AZULEJOS: Spanish and Portuguese word for 'tiles'.

BARBOTINE: Decoration of coloured slip applied by trailer, brush or spatula.

BAT: A gelatine pad sometimes used in the process of transfer-printing.

BIANCO-SOPRA-BIANCO: Italian for 'white-on-white' and to be found on tin-glazed tiles, particularly those made in Bristol during the 18th century.

BISCUIT: A tile that has been fired once. It is the biscuit tile that is glazed and decorated.

BODY: Main substance of a tile.

CERAMIC COLOUR: A pigment that will withstand the fierce heat of the kiln.

CHINOISERIE: A name given to 18th and 19th century objects and patterns that show design influences from the Far East.

CLASSICISM: A term used throughout the visual arts to denote the influence of Greek and Roman art and design.

COADE STONE: A fired clay body which was much used for architectural detailing and ornament at the end of the 18th and the beginning of the 19th centuries. Named after Mrs Eleanor Coade who founded Coade's Artificial Stone Works, Lambeth, London. Apart from architectural ornament, urns, tombs, statues and garden objects were made.

COBALT: A metal oxide which produces a strong blue colour when fired in the kiln. Much used for the decoration of tin-glazed tiles and later printed blue-and-white tiles.

CUENCA TILE: A Spanish tile with a moulded design with raised edges. Into each cavity different coloured glazes could be introduced (*cuenca* means 'bowl' in Spanish).

CUERDA SECA TILE: A Spanish tile with a design first painted in outline using a compound of iron-oxide and grease. Further colours can be added, rapidly painted on because they retreat from the grease and do not overlap. The outlines after firing show as matt black between glossy colours (*cuerda seca* means 'dry cord' in Spanish).

DELFTWARE TILE: Tile dipped in tin-glaze at biscuit stage on which a decoration is painted by hand. This decoration is called 'in-glaze' because it sinks into the tin-glaze during the second firing. The term 'delftware' is derived from the Dutch town of Delft.

DUST-CLAY: Finely powdered clay with a low moisture content.

DUST-PRESSING: The compressing with great force of powdered clay.

ÉMAUX OMBRANTS: A relief tile finished with a single translucent coloured glaze. Pooling in the hollows produces gradations of great delicacy.

ENAMEL: A ceramic colour which can be painted on a glazed tile and be permanently fixed to it by means of low temperature firing in a muffle kiln.

ENCAUSTIC TILE: A ceramic tile in which a pattern or figurative motif is inlaid with coloured clays into the main body of the tile.

ENGOBE: Liquid clay applied to the tile body as decoration.

FAIENCE: Originally a term for tin-glazed ware, but during the 19th century it was used to indicate architectural ceramics that had been moulded and glazed. The word comes from the name of the Italian town Faenza.

HISPANO-MORESQUE: A term used for pottery and tiles produced in Spain during the 14th and 15th centuries under Moorish influence in places such as Malaga and Valencia. It is characterized by the use of lustre often in combination with cobalt blue on a white tin-glaze.

IN-GLAZE: *See* 'Delftware Tile'.

INTAGLIO: Relief in reverse.

ISLAM: Term for the Mohammedan religion and culture whose origins go back to AD 622 when it was founded by the prophet Mohammed. Other terms synonymous with this are 'Moslem' and 'Muslim'. The tiles produced in the Middle East under its influence are normally referred to as 'Islamic'.

KILN: Oven in which pottery and tiles are fired.

LEAD GLAZE: Glassy, transparent glaze made from lead oxide and therefore highly poisonous in an unfired state.

LUSTRE: A ceramic colour that through the introduction of smoke into the kiln during firing turns into a thin film of metal. Copper and silver lustre are the most common.

MAIOLICA/MAJOLICA: Originally earthenware with white tin-glaze painted in bright colours, but the term spelled as 'majolica' was also used in the 19th century for relief tiles and pottery with colourful opaque glazes. The word comes from the name of Majorca, the island which used to be a major centre of painted pottery during the 15th century.

MANGANESE: A metal oxide producing mauve.

MASTER DESIGN: Original design from which copies are taken.

MOORISH CULTURE: Arabs who occupied parts of southern Spain between 711 and 1492 developed a distinctive culture in which tiles and pottery featured prominently. *See also* 'Hispano-Moresque'.

MOSAIC: Small pieces of glass, stone or fired clay arranged to make a pattern or picture and cemented to wall or floor.

MUFFLE KILN: A special kiln with a refractory internal shell which protects the ware from the direct flame and combustion gases. In the case of tiles it is used for firing on-glaze decorations.

NEO-GOTHIC: The revival of medieval design in the 19th century. A W N Pugin was the major architect and tile designer in Britain of this style.

ON-GLAZE: Decoration executed on the glaze with enamels. Because on-glaze decoration can be fired at a lower temperature, a more varied palette of colours is available than with under-glaze decoration.

OPUS SECTILE: A Latin term that indicates pieces cut into shapes which follow the lines of the pattern or picture.

PÂTE-SUR-PÂTE: A French term meaning 'paste-on-paste'. A delicate form of low-relief decoration built up by layer on layer of white slip on a contrasting ground. Louis Marc Solon, who worked for Minton between 1870 and 1904, was the outstanding artist of this technique.

PLASTIC CLAY: Ordinary wet clay.

POUNCE: Little cloth bag filled with black powder which is patted over a perforated drawing for getting a design on a tile. The little dots serve as a guide for hand-painting. Much used for the decoration of 'majolica' and 'delftware', or tiles with slip-trailed designs.

QUARRY TILE: A plain square floor tile resistant to heavy abrasion.

REGISTRATION MARK: A diamond shaped mark with letters and numbers that denote the day, month and year of registering the design as well as the 'class' (metal, wood, pottery, etc.) and a 'parcel number' which identifies a particular register entry. From February 1884 a simple registration number was used. It provided manufacturers with protection against their designs being copied.

RELIEF: Raised design.

SGRAFFITO: Scratching through the top surface of two layers of clay and revealing the colour of the bottom layer. From the Latin *grafitto* meaning 'scratching'.

SLIP: Thin liquid clay.

STENCIL: A piece of paper, cardboard or metal with a design cut out of it through which colour can be applied.

STOVE TILES: Glazed tiles that formed part of large free-standing ceramic stoves common in Germany, Austria and Switzerland, a tradition that goes back at least to the 15th century in that part of Europe. They usually have moulded relief designs for increased heat radiation. Making stove tiles was the work of specialist craftsmen. Nuremberg was a major production centre.

TERRACOTTA: Italian for 'baked earth'. The term is now normally used for unglazed architectural ceramics.

TILE BLANK: A formed tile before it has received any sort of decoration.

TIN-GLAZE: A glaze made by adding tin to a lead glaze which, when fired, becomes an opaque white.

TRANSFER-PRINTING: The transfer of a printed image from a metal plate, wood-block or lithographic stone by means of thin paper or gelatinous 'bats' to the surface of pottery and tiles. Transfer-printing can be over-glaze or under-glaze. This technique was first used for tiles in 1756 by the printer John Sadler, of Liverpool.

TRANSLUCENT GLAZE: A transparent glaze to which colour has been added, allowing the surface to which it has been applied to show through.

TUBE-LINING: The piping of delicate lines of slip on to pottery and tiles to form raised lines that separated areas of coloured glazes.

UNDER-GLAZE: A printed or painted decoration under a transparent glaze. Because the decoration is covered by a glaze it is completely durable. The transparent glaze has to be fired at a high temperature and the range of available colours for under-glaze decoration is therefore limited.

GENERAL BIBLIOGRAPHY

J & B Austwick *The Decorated Tile*, Pitman House, London 1980

J Barnard *Victorian Ceramic Tiles*, Studio Vista/Christies, London 1972

M Batkin *Wedgwood Ceramics 1846–1959*, Richard Dennis Publications,
        Shepton Beauchamp 1982

K Beaulah *Church Tiles of the Nineteenth Century*, Shire Publications,
        Princes Risborough 1987

A Berendsen *Tiles – A General History*, Faber & Faber, London 1967

J Catleugh *William De Morgan Tiles*, Trefoil, London 1983

A J Cross *Pilkington's Royal Lancastrian Pottery and Tiles*, Richard Dennis Publications,
        London 1980

E S Eames *Medieval Tiles – A Handbook*, British Museum, London 1968

E S Eames *English Medieval Tiles*, British Museum Publications, London 1985

W J Furnival *Leadless Decorative Tiles, Faience and Mosaic*, Furnival (privately published),
        Stone 1904

W G Gaunt & M D E Clayton-Stamm *William De Morgan*, Studio Vista, London 1971

J Greene *Brightening the Long Days: Hospital Tile Pictures*, Tiles & Architectural Ceramics
        Society/Alan Sutton Publishing, Gloucester 1987

M Greenwood *Designs of William De Morgan*, Richard Dennis, Shepton Beauchamp 1989

D Hamilton *Architectural Ceramics*, Thames & Hudson, London 1978

J Hawkins *The Poole Potteries*, Barrie and Jenkins, London 1980

T Herbert *The Jackfield Decorative Tile Industry*, Ironbridge Gorge Museum Trust,
        Ironbridge 1978

J Horne *English Tin-Glazed Tiles*, J Horne Antiques Ltd, London 1989

L Jewitt *Ceramic Art of Great Britain*, 2 Vols, Virtue & Co, London 1878

C H de Jonge *Dutch Tiles*, Pall Mall Press, London 1971

A Kelly *Mrs Coade's Stone*, Self Publishing Association Ltd, Upton-upon-Severn 1990
D Korf *Dutch Tiles*, Merlin Press, London 1963
L Lambton *An Album of Curious Houses*, Chatto & Windus, London 1988
A Lane *A Guide to the Collection of Tiles*, Victoria and Albert Museum, London 1939
H van Lemmen *Victorian Tiles*, Shire Publications, Princes Risborough 1981
H van Lemmen *Delftware Tiles*, Shire Publications, Princes Risborough 1986
H van Lemmen *Decorative Tiles Throughout the Ages*, Bracken Books, 1988
H van Lemmen *Tiled Furniture*, Shire Publications, Princes Risborough 1989
H van Lemmen *Tiles – A Collector's Guide*, Souvenir Press, London 1990
T Lockett *Collecting Victorian Tiles*, Antique Collectors' Club, Woodbridge 1979
J Meco *Azulejos: The Stunning Tile Heritage of Portugal*, Barbican Centre with the
        Anglo-Portuguese Foundation, London 1986
M Messenger *Pottery and Tiles of the Severn Valley*, Remploy, London 1979
T Paul *Tiles for a Beautiful Home,* Merehurst Press, London 1989
R Pinkham *Catalogue of Pottery by William De Morgan*, Victoria and Albert Museum,
        London 1973
B Rackham *Early Netherlands Maiolica*, London 1926
A Ray *English Delftware Tiles*, Faber & Faber, London 1973
N Riley *Tile Art*, Quintet, 1987
D S Skinner & H van Lemmen *Minton Tiles 1835–1935*, Stoke-on-Trent City Museum
        & Art Gallery, 1984
J Wight *Mediaeval Floor Tiles*, John Baker, London 1975

THE CATALOGUE

A set of tiled letters by Minton, Hollins &
Co, formerly inside Jackson's Restaurant,
Paragon Street, Kingston-upon-Hull.
(Private collection.)

83

FOREWORD

To celebrate the 10th anniversary of the founding of the Tiles & Architectural Ceramics Society, Scarborough Borough Council was asked to organize a comprehensive exhibition of tiles, showing their historical context and development throughout Europe from medieval times, through the peak of Victorian tile making in England to contemporary activity in tile design and manufacture today.

The resulting exhibition is probably the largest and most varied exhibition of tiles to be seen in Britain so far. It has brought together tiles from most of the country's major public and private collections, and includes some which have never been exhibited before. Many are rare and unique examples, produced in a tile manufacturing past and their glory may never be achieved again in quite the same way.

It is hoped that the exhibition will inspire and encourage our contemporary designers, craft workers and manufacturers to re-establish the work of enriching our buildings with colour and decorative form which has sadly been missed in recent decades. Now is as good a time as any to see a strong and decisive revival of tiles and architectural ceramics of all kinds. ❧

Josie Montgomery
CURATOR OF ART
SCARBOROUGH ART GALLERY

ISLAMIC
TILES

1

2

3

4

5

6

7

8

MEDIEVAL TILES

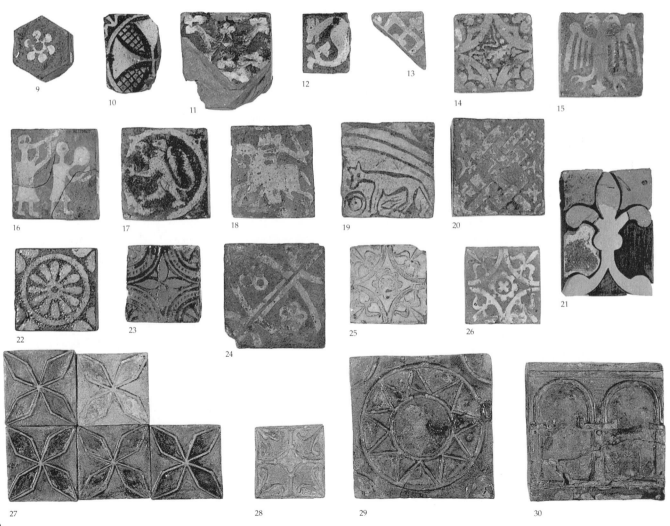

9

10

11

12

13

14

15

16

17

18

19

20

21

22

23

24

25

26

27

28

29

30

31

32

33

34

Tin-Glazed Tiles

35

36

37

38

39

40

41

42

43

44

45

46

47

48

49

50

51

52

53

54

55

56

57

58

59

60

61

62

63

64

65

66

67

68

69

70

71

72

73

74

75

76

77

78

79

80

81

82

83

84

85

86

87

88

89

90

91

92

93

94

95

96

97

98

99

100

101

102

103

104

105

106

107

108

109

110

111

112

113

114

115

116

117

118

119

120

121

122

123

124

125

126

127

128

129

GOTHIC REVIVAL TILES

130

131

132

133

134

135

136

137

138

139

140

141

142

143

144

145

146

147

148

149

150

151

152

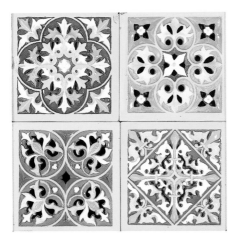

153

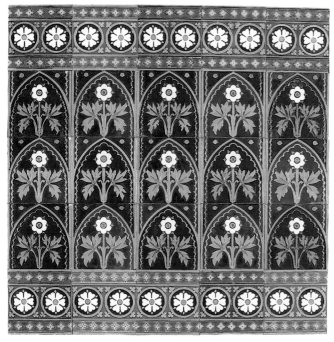

154

155

156

157

158

159

160

161

162

163

164

MINTON TILES

165

166

167

168

169

170

171

172

173

174

175

176

177

178

179

180

181

182

183

184

185

186

187

188

189

190

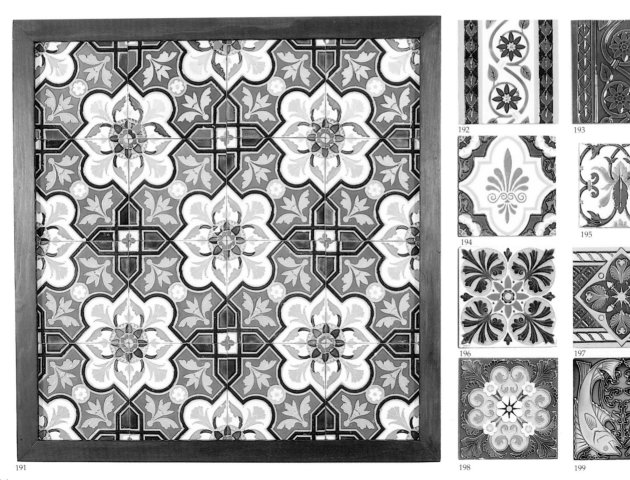

191

192

193

194

195

196

197

198

199

200

201

202

203

204

205

206

207

208

209

210

211

212

213

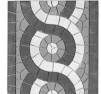

214

215

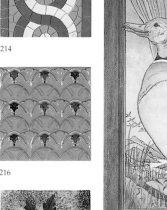

216

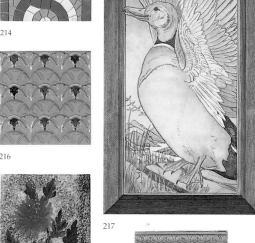

217

218

219

220

221

222

223

224

225

226

227

228

229

230

231

232

233

234

235

236

237

238

CRAVEN DUNNILL TILES

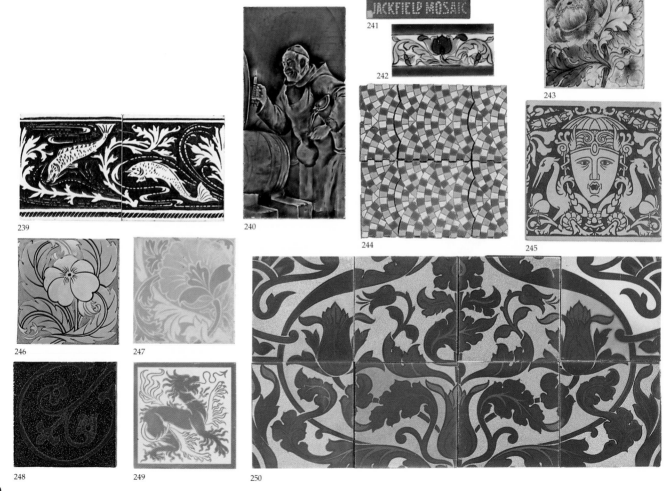

239

240

241

CRAVEN DUNNILL
JACKFIELD MOSAIC

242

243

244

245

246

247

248

249

250

WEDGWOOD
TILES

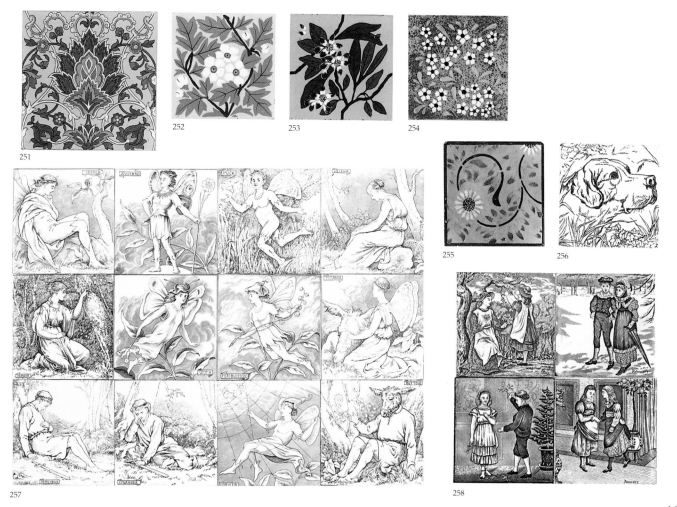

251

252

253

254

255

256

257

258

DOULTON TILES

259

260

261

263

264

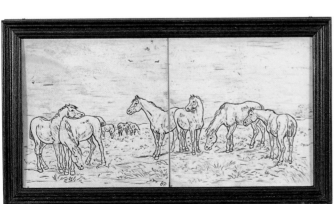

262

265

PILKINGTON TILES AND MARTIN BROTHERS TILES

266

267

268

269

274

275

270

271

272

273

276

277

BURMANTOFTS TILES

278

279

280

281

282

283

284

285

286

287

288

289

290

291

292

293

294

SIMPSON
TILES

296

295

297

298

299

300

301

302

303

304

305

306

307

308

309

310

311

312

313

314

315

OTHER TILEMAKERS

316

317

318

319

320

321

322

323

324

325

326

327

328

329

330

ART NOUVEAU TILES

331

332

333

334

335

336

337

338

339

340

341

342

343

121

MORRIS & CO TILES

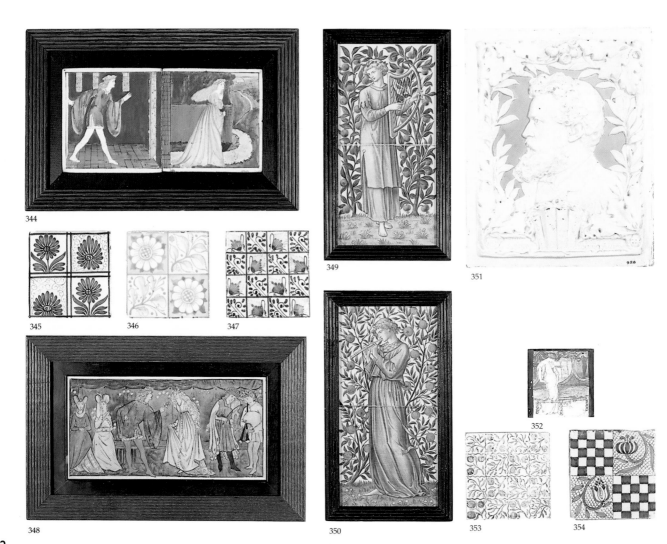

344

345   346   347

348

349

350

351

352

353   354

355

356

357

358

359

360

361

362

363

WILLIAM DE MORGAN TILES

364

366

367

368

369

370

371

372

373

374

375

376

377

378

TILE DESIGNERS

379

380

381

382

383

384

385

386

387

388

389

TILE DESIGNERS

379

380

381

382

383

384

385

386

387

388

389

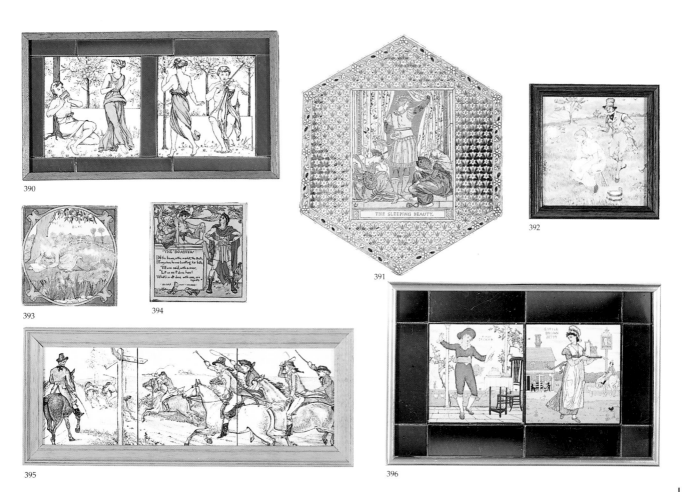

390

391

392

393

394

395

396

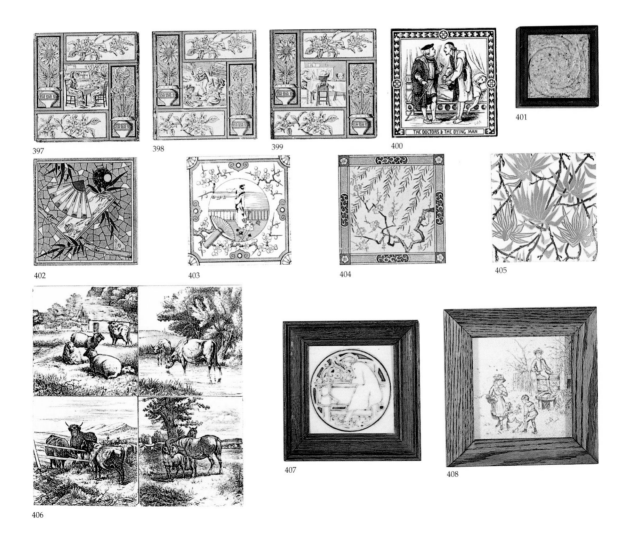

397

398

399

400

401

402

403

404

405

406

407

408

409

410

411

412

413

414

415

416

417

418

Tiles
In
Use

419

420

421

422

423

424

425

426

427

428

429

EUROPEAN TILES

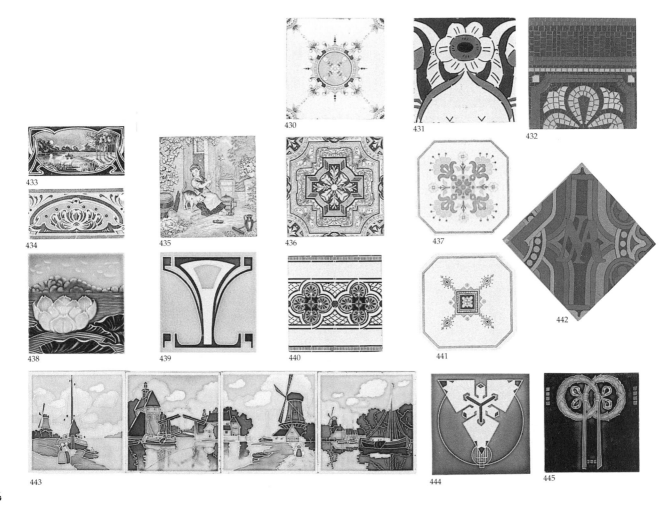

430

431

432

433

434

435

436

437

438

439

440

441

442

443

444

445

446

447

448

449

450

451

452

453

454

455

456

457

458

20TH CENTURY BRITISH TILES

459

460

461

462

463

464

465

466

467

468

469

470

471

472

473

474

475

476

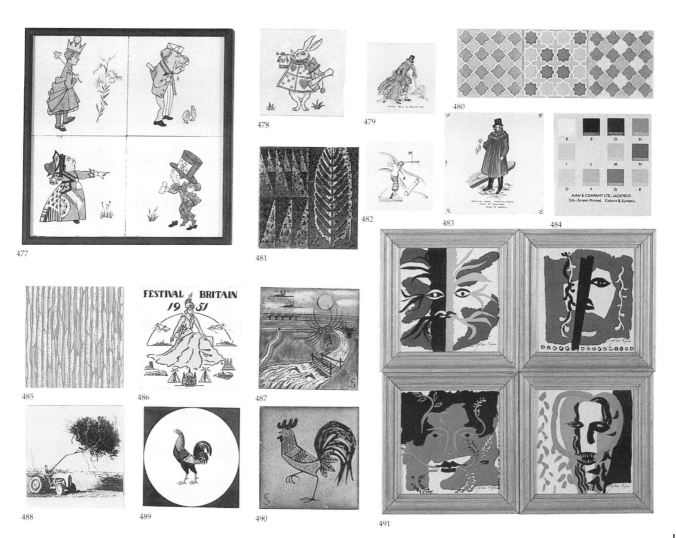

477

478

479

480

481

482

483

484

485

486

487

488

489

490

491

CONTEMPORARY
TILES

492

493

494

495

496

497

498

499

500

501

502

503

504

505

513

506

507

508

509

510

511

512

514

515

516

517

518

519

520

521

522

523

524

ISLAMIC TILES

1 Tile with hand-painted under-glaze floral decoration in turquoise, blue, green and black.
Plastic clay, 230 x 230mm.
Damascus, Syria, 16th or 17th century.
City Museum & Art Gallery,
Stoke-on-Trent (formerly in the collection
of Lord Leighton).

2 Three tile fragments, hand-painted in yellow lustre.
Plastic clay.
Persian, 13th century.
Private collection.

3 Four tiles with relief-moulded and hand-painted in-glaze floral decoration in purple, turquoise, blue and black.
Plastic clay, each tile 213 x 213mm.
Possibly Persian, 14th century.
City Museum & Art Gallery,
Stoke-on-Trent.

4 Tile with relief-moulded and hand-painted decoration in blue with yellow lustre.
Part of a frieze with an Arabic inscription.
Plastic clay, 430 x 385mm.
Kashan (Persia), 13th or 14th century.
City Museum & Art Gallery,
Stoke-on-Trent.

5 Detail from a panel of 55 tiles, hand-painted in-glaze decoration depicting Islamic architectural and floral motifs in yellow, blue, green and purple.
Plastic clay, each tile 155 x 155mm.
Tunisia, 19th century.
City Museum & Art Gallery,
Stoke-on-Trent.

6 Tile with hand-painted under-glaze floral decoration in turquoise, green, blue and black.
Plastic clay, 230 x 230mm.
Damascus, Syria, 16th or 17th century.
City Museum & Art Gallery,
Stoke-on-Trent.

7 Four tiles with relief-moulded and hand-painted floral decoration in blue, pink, turquoise and black.
Plastic clay, each tile 310 x 310mm.
Persian, late-19th century.
City Museum & Art Gallery,
Stoke-on-Trent.

8 Two tiles with hand-painted under-glaze floral motifs in blue and turquoise.
Plastic clay, each tile 250 x 250mm.
Turkish, 17th century.
City Museum & Art Gallery,
Stoke-on-Trent.

MEDIEVAL TILES

9 Lead-glazed inlaid tile with a design of a small six-petalled flower.
Plastic clay, 75mm across.
Byland Abbey, Yorkshire, *c.*1200.
Private collection.

10 Hand-coloured inlaid tile fragment with part of a Maltese Cross within an encircling band and the arms probably for Warrenne. Plastic clay.
Nottingham kiln, 14th century.
Private collection.

11 Lead-glazed inlaid tile fragment. The device of trefoil-ended cusps is overlaid with a smaller shape of the same, a quatrefoil in the centre.
Plastic clay, full size 124 x 124mm.
Site of the church of Meaux Abbey, Yorkshire, late-15th century.
Private collection.

12 Lead-glazed inlaid tile fragment depicting part of a griffin.
Plastic clay, full size 80 x 80mm.
Clarendon Palace, Wiltshire, 1242.
Private collection.

13 Lead-glazed inlaid tile fragment with a geometric design.
Plastic clay, full size 750 x 750mm.
Clarendon Palace, Wiltshire, 1242.
Private collection.

14 Lead-glazed inlaid tile depicting a lion rampant between four quadrants. Plastic clay, 105 x 105mm. Teynsham Church, Kent, mid-14th century. *Private collection.*

15 Lead-glazed inlaid tile of a double-headed eagle. Plastic clay, 110 x 110mm. Watton Priory, Driffield, Humberside, c.1280. *Private collection.*

16 Lead-glazed inlaid tile depicting a 'two-man band'. One beats percussion, the other blows a horn. Plastic clay, 110 x 110mm. Watton Priory, Driffield, Humberside, c.1280. *Private collection.*

17 Lead-glazed inlaid floor tile depicting a lion rampant within an encircling band. Plastic clay, 117 x 117mm. Haughmond Priory, Shropshire, 13th century. *Private collection.*

18 Lead-glazed inlaid tile of a knight on horseback with a sword and shield. Plastic clay, 112 x 112mm. Dunstable Priory, 13th century. *Private collection.*

19 Tile depicting a medieval fable of a tiger being diverted by a mirror. Plastic clay, 122 x 122mm. Meaux Abbey, Yorkshire, late-15th century. *Private collection.*

20 Lead-glazed inlaid tile with geometric strapwork. Plastic clay, 125 x 125mm. Harpsden Church, Henley-on-Thames, Oxfordshire. Tyler's Green (Penn, Buckinghamshire) kiln, late-13th century. *Private collection.*

21 Small mosaic panel (restored) of six pieces forming a fleur-de-lis. Plastic clay, 165 x 120mm. Meaux Abbey, Yorkshire, c.1250. *Private collection.*

22 Lead-glazed inlaid tile of a daisy within a circle with petal-shaped corner motifs. Plastic clay, 110 x 110mm. Thornton Abbey, South Humberside, c.1300. *Private collection.*

23 Lead-glazed impressed tile with a geometric pattern. Plastic clay, 100 x 100mm. Whalley Abbey, Lancashire, c.1380. *Private collection.*

24 Lead-glazed inlaid tile with geometric motifs. Plastic clay, 139 x 139mm. Combermere Abbey, Cheshire, 13th century. *Private collection.*

25–26 Two impressed tiles covered with white engobe depicting the same design from the same stamp, but the white engobe on No 26 has worn off the surface of the tile revealing the red surface which now contrasts with the engobe-covered motif of No 27. These two tiles illustrate a possible origin of the two-coloured inlaid tile, i.e. to obtain this effect by scraping off the white engobe. Plastic clay, each tile 112 x 112mm. Meaux Abbey, Yorkshire, c.1250. *Private collection.*

27 Five lead-glazed late-Saxon tiles with a geometric design of lozenges with raised outlines. Plastic clay, 950 x 950mm. All Saints Church, York, 10th century. *The Yorkshire Museum, York and private collection.*

28 Lead-glazed late-Saxon tile with a geometric motif with raised outlines. Plastic clay, 950 x 950mm. All Saints Church, York, 10th century. *Private collection.*

29 Lead-glazed late-Saxon tile with a circular geometric motif with raised outlines.
Plastic clay, 185 x 185mm.
All Saints Church, York, 10th century.
The Yorkshire Museum, York.

30 Lead-glazed late-Saxon tile with an architectural motif of two round-headed arches with raised outlines.
Plastic clay, 180 x 180mm.
All Saints Church, York, 10th century.
The Yorkshire Museum, York.

31 Four lead-glazed inlaid tiles. The words 'AVE MARIA' (Hail Mary) are repeated to form a circle, each tile having a heart-shaped petal to form a central flower.
Plastic clay, each tile 124 x 124mm.
From the church of Meaux Abbey, Yorkshire, late-15th century.
Private collection.

32 Eight lead-glazed inlaid tiles being half of a 16-tile setting, with a centre circle made of four fleurs-de-lis surrounded by three bands depicting florettes, dragons or 'worms' and running scroll motifs.
Plastic clay. Château de Chaourse, France, mid-14th century
Private collection.

33 Geometric tile mosaic of 12 pieces forming a six-petalled flower, each piece cut by hand with the aid of templates.
Plastic clay, *c.*1250.
Private collection.

34 Five lead-glazed inlaid tiles and four plain tiles. Design of four-leaved palmettes, the centre tile carries the pattern in four directions being the intersection of decorated bands enclosing four (or more) plain tiles.
Plastic clay, each tile 114 x 114mm.
Watton Priory, Driffield, Humberside, late-13th century.
Private collection.

TIN-GLAZED TILES

35 Four tin-glazed tiles with hand-painted in-glaze decoration of stylized floral designs. Blue and orange.
Plastic clay, each tile 130 x 130mm.
Spanish, 16th century.
Private collection.

36 Two tin-glazed tiles with hand-painted in-glaze decoration of stylized flowers and leaves.
Plastic clay, each tile 130 x 130mm.
Spanish, 16th century.
Private collection.

37 Tin-glazed tile with hand-painted in-glaze decoration with a floral design. Polychrome.
Plastic clay, 130 x 130mm.
Spanish, 16th century.
Private collection.

38 Tin-glazed tile with hand-painted in-glaze decoration with a stylized floral motif. Polychrome.
Plastic clay, 130 x 130mm.
Spanish, 16th century.
Private collection.

39 Tin-glazed tile with hand-painted in-glaze decoration depicting a camel. Blue, green and orange.
Plastic clay, 130 x 130mm.
Dutch, early-17th century.
Private collection.

40 Tin-glazed tile with hand-painted in-glaze decoration of a floral design. Blue, orange and green.
Plastic clay, 132 x 132mm.
Dutch, *c.*1600.
Private collection.

41 Tin-glazed tile with hand-painted in-glaze decoration of a 'star tulip' surrounded by a pomegranate and grape design.. Polychrome.
Plastic clay, 130 x 130mm.
Dutch, *c.*1620.
Private collection.

42 Tin-glazed tile with hand-painted in-glaze decoration of a central flower within a quadrant. Orange and green. 'Reserve' corner motif in blue.
Plastic clay, 130 x 130mm.
Dutch, *c*.1620.
Private collection.

43 Tin-glazed tile with hand-painted in-glaze decoration of a bird. Ox-head corners. Orange and blue.
Plastic clay, 130 x 130mm. Dutch, *c*.1625.
Private collection.

44 Tin-glazed tile with hand-painted in-glaze decoration of a carnation. Bold fleur-de-lis corner motifs. Orange, blue and green.
Plastic clay, 130 x 130mm.
Dutch, *c*.1635–70.
Private collection.

45 Tin-glazed tile with hand-painted in-glaze decoration depicting a Turkish warrior. Green and orange.
Plastic clay, 128 x 128mm.
Dutch, *c*.1600–25.
Private collection.

46 Tin-glazed tile with hand-painted in-glaze decoration depicting three tulips in a scalloped border. Wan li corners. Blue, green and orange.
Plastic clay, 130 x 130mm. Dutch, *c*.1625.
Private collection.

47 Tin-glazed tile with hand-painted in-glaze decoration depicting a soldier. The border is formed by four 'accolades'. Blue.
Plastic clay, 130 x 130mm.
Dutch, *c*.1625–50.
Private collection.

48 Tin-glazed tile with hand-painted in-glaze decoration depicting a dog, set within a candelabra border. Blue.
Plastic clay, 130 x 130mm.
Dutch, *c*.1620.
Private collection.

49 Tin-glazed tile with hand-painted in-glaze decoration depicting a bagpiper. Blue.
Plastic clay, 130 x 130mm.
Dutch, *c*.1640.
Private collection.

50 Tin-glazed tile with hand-painted in-glaze decoration of an elephant in a scalloped Wan li border. Blue.
Plastic clay, 120 x 120mm.
Dutch, *c*.1625.
Private collection.

51 Tin-glazed tile with hand-painted in-glaze decoration depicting a vase with flowers. Ox-head corners. Blue.
Plastic clay, 120 x 120mm.
Dutch, *c*.1650.
Private collection.

52 Tin-glazed tile with hand-painted in-glaze decoration of a well and sailing boats. Spider-head corners. Blue.
Plastic clay, 125 x 125mm.
Dutch, *c*.1650–1700.
Private collection.

53 Tin-glazed tile with hand-painted in-glaze decoration depicting a cupid. Spider-head corners. Blue.
Plastic clay, 126 x 126mm.
Dutch, *c*.1650–1700.
Private collection.

54 Tin-glazed tile with hand-painted in-glaze decoration depicting a bridge with two figures and three boats. Spider-head corners. Blue.
Plastic clay, 126 x 126mm.
Dutch, *c*.1650–1700.
Private collection.

55 Tin-glazed tile with hand-painted in-glaze decoration of a man in a landscape within a circle. Ox-head corners. Blue.
Plastic clay, 125 x 125mm. Dutch, *c*.1700.
Private collection.

56 Tin-glazed tile with hand-painted in-glaze decoration depicting three boats and a causeway with a tower. Ox-head corners. Blue.
Plastic clay, 125 x 125mm. Dutch, *c*.1750.
Private collection.

57 Tin-glazed tile with hand-painted in-glaze decoration depicting a herdsman with two cattle. Purple central design. Blue border.
Plastic clay, 130 x 130mm.
Dutch, *c.*1750.
Glasgow Museums & Art Galleries.

58 Tin-glazed tile with hand-painted in-glaze decoration depicting a stallholder. Blue.
Plastic clay, 125 x 125mm.
Dutch, *c.*1750.
Private collection.

59 Six tin-glazed tiles with hand-painted in-glaze decoration depicting biblical scenes.
Plastic clay, each tile 130 x 130mm, *c.*1750.
[These tiles are normally kept at the People's Palace, Glasgow, where they are ascribed to the Delftfield Pottery (1748–1832) in Glasgow. It is more probable, however, that they are 18th century Dutch tiles from Rotterdam.]
Glasgow Museums & Art Galleries.

60 Tin-glazed tile with hand-painted in-glaze decoration depicting a boatman taking cattle across a river. Cherub border. Dark blue.
Plastic clay, 130 x 130mm.
Liverpool, *c.*1750–75.
Liverpool Museum.

61 Tin-glazed tile with hand-painted in-glaze decoration of *Moses receiving the Tablets.* Blue.
Plastic clay, 130 x 130mm.
Liverpool, *c.*1750–70.
Liverpool Museum.

62 Tin-glazed tile with hand-painted in-glaze decoration of a lady with a cloak in a landscape setting. Louis XV border with buttercup corners. Blue.
Plastic clay, 126 x 126mm.
Liverpool, *c.*1750–80.
Liverpool Museum.

63 Tin-glazed tile with hand-painted in-glaze decoration of a house beside a fence. Studded border. Dark blue.
Plastic clay, 125 x 125mm.
Liverpool, *c.*1750–70.
Liverpool Museum.

64 Tin-glazed tile with hand-painted in-glaze decoration of grapes and vine leaves. Green and purple.
Plastic clay, 128 x 128mm.
Liverpool, *c.*1775–1800.
Liverpool Museum.

65 Tin-glazed tile with hand-painted in-glaze decoration depicting a butterfly. Orange and blue.
Plastic clay, 128 x 128mm.
Liverpool or Bristol, *c.*1750–75.
Liverpool Museum.

66 Tin-glazed tile with hand-painted in-glaze decoration of a chinoiserie figure. Purple with *bianco-sopra-bianco* border.
Plastic clay, 124 x 124mm.
Liverpool or Bristol, *c.*1760–70.
Liverpool Museum.

67 Tin-glazed tile with hand-painted in-glaze decoration depicting a floral display in a vase. Fazackerly colours with a *bianco-sopra-bianco* border.
Plastic clay, 128 x 128mm.
Liverpool, *c.*1770.
Private collection.

68 Tin-glazed tile with hand-painted in-glaze decoration of stylized flowers over a cartouche. Cupid corners. Dark blue.
Plastic clay, 126 x 126mm.
Liverpool, *c.*1750–75.
Liverpool Museum.

69 Tin-glazed tile with hand-painted in-glaze decoration of *Jesus and the Woman of Samaria.* Purple.
Plastic clay, 128 x 128mm.
Liverpool, *c.*1740–60.
Liverpool Museum.

70 Tin-glazed tile with hand-painted in-glaze decoration depicting a heron. Fazackerly colours.
Plastic clay, 128 x 128mm.
Liverpool, *c.*1750–70.
Liverpool Museum.

71 Tin-glazed tile with hand-painted in-glaze decoration of a couple walking. Orange and blue.
Plastic clay, 125 x 125mm.
Liverpool, c.1755–75.
Liverpool Museum.

72 Tin-glazed tile with hand-painted in-glaze decoration of a man chopping wood. Barred ox-head corners. Purple.
Plastic clay, 126 x 126mm.
Liverpool, c.1750–70.
Liverpool Museum.

73 Tin-glazed tile with hand-painted in-glaze decoration of a landscape scene. Dandelion corners. Blue and purple.
Plastic clay, 125 x 125mm.
Liverpool, c.1740–60.
Liverpool Museum.

74 Tin-glazed tile with hand-painted in-glaze decoration of a vase of flowers. Fazackerly colours.
Plastic clay, 128 x 128mm.
Liverpool, c.1760–75.
Liverpool Museum.

75 Tin-glazed tile with hand-painted in-glaze decoration of a Chinese figure holding out his hand. Fish roe border and daisy corners. Polychrome.
Plastic clay, 127 x 127mm.
Liverpool, c.1750–70.
Liverpool Museum.

76 Tin-glazed edging tile with hand-painted in-glaze decoration, running foliage and flowers. Dark blue.
Plastic clay, 129 x 50mm.
London or Liverpool, c.1760–80.
Liverpool Museum.

77 Tin-glazed edging tile with hand-painted in-glaze decoration of a running grape vine. Green and purple.
Plastic clay, 127 x 60mm.
Liverpool or Bristol, c.1750–75.
Liverpool Museum.

78 Tin-glazed tile with wood-block printed on-glaze decoration depicting a girl seated in a landscape. Purple.
Plastic clay, 129 x 129mm.
Sadler and Green, Liverpool, c.1756–57.
Liverpool Museum.

79 Tin-glazed tile with wood-block printed on-glaze decoration depicting a hunter and a huntress by a fountain. Blue.
Plastic clay, 128 x 128mm.
Sadler and Green, Liverpool, c.1756–57.
Liverpool Museum.

80 Tin-glazed tile with wood-block printed on-glaze decoration of a shepherdess and her swain.
Plastic clay, 128 x 128mm.
Sadler and Green, Liverpool, c.1756–57.
Private collection.

81 Tin-glazed tile with copper-plate printed on-glaze decoration of the *Crow with the Pitcher*. Black.
Plastic clay, 125 x 125mm.
Sadler and Green, Liverpool, c.1775.
Liverpool Museum.

82 Tin-glazed tile with copper-plate printed on-glaze decoration depicting harvest figures in an oval design. Hand-stencilled tinting. Black with green.
Plastic clay, 126 x 126mm.
Sadler and Green, Liverpool, c.1775.
Private collection.

83 Tin-glazed tile with copper-plate printed on-glaze decoration of the *Three Graces*. Black with green.
Plastic clay, 126 x 126mm.
Sadler and Green, Liverpool, c.1775.
Private collection.

84 Tin-glazed tile with copper-plate printed on-glaze decoration depicting a Classical urn. Black with green enamel.
Plastic clay, 125 x 125mm.
Sadler and Green, Liverpool, c.1775.
Private collection.

85 Tin-glazed tile with copper-plate printed on-glaze decoration depicting a couple by a windmill. Brown.
Plastic clay, 125 x 125mm.
Sadler and Green, Liverpool, c.1770.
Liverpool Museum.

86 Tin-glazed tile with copper-plate printed on-glaze decoration depicting a rustic couple with a dog. Brown. Plastic clay, 125 x 125mm. Sadler and Green, Liverpool, *c*.1760. *Liverpool Museum.*

87 Tin-glazed tile with copper-plate printed on-glaze decoration depicting a boy watching a girl blow bubbles. Black. Plastic clay, 125 x 125mm. Sadler and Green, Liverpool, *c*.1765. *Liverpool Museum.*

88 Tin-glazed tile with copper-plate printed on-glaze decoration of a man putting on a girl's skate. Black. Plastic clay, 125 x 125mm. Sadler and Green, Liverpool, *c*.1760. *Liverpool Museum.*

89 Tin-glazed tile with copper-plate printed on-glaze decoration of a fortune-teller and a girl with a rake. Black. Plastic clay, 125 x 125mm. Sadler and Green, Liverpool, *c*.1770. *Liverpool Museum.*

90 Tin-glazed tile with hand-stencilled in-glaze decoration depicting a geometric layout around a central motif. Polychrome. Plastic clay, 203 x 203mm. Spanish, *c*.1890. *Private collection.*

91 Tin-glazed tile with hand-painted in-glaze decoration depicting a horseman. Orange and blue. Plastic clay, 132 x 132mm. Italian, 20th century. *Private collection.*

92 Tin-glazed tile with hand-painted in-glaze decoration depicting a sailing ship. Orange and blue. Plastic clay, 132 x 132mm. Spanish, *c*.1800. *Private collection.*

93 Tin-glazed tile with hand-painted in-glaze decoration of *Don Quixote with Sancho Panza*. Orange and pale green. Plastic clay, 130 x 130mm. Spanish, 20th century. *Private collection.*

94 Tin-glazed tile with hand-stencilled in-glaze decoration depicting a geometric layout. Polychrome. Plastic clay, 203 x 203mm. Spanish, *c*.1890. *Private collection.*

95 Tin-glazed tile with hand-stencilled in-glaze decoration depicting a geometric four square design. Orange, ochre and blue. Plastic clay, 203 x 203mm. Spanish, *c*.1890. *Private collection.*

96 Four tin-glazed tiles with hand-stencilled in-glaze decoration. Rose-head corners. Plastic clay, each tile 203 x 203mm. Spanish, *c*.1890. *Private collection.*

97 Tin-glazed tile with hand-painted in-glaze decoration of a bird on a bough within a square. Blue and green. Plastic clay, 203 x 203mm. Italian, 19th century. *Private collection.*

98 Tin-glazed tile with stencilled in-glaze decoration in a four square design of stylized flowers. Blue and orange. Plastic clay, 203 x 203mm. Spanish, *c*.1900. *Private collection.*

99 Tin-glazed tile with hand-stencilled in-glaze decoration depicting a central floral design. Pink and green. Plastic clay, 152 x 152mm. Spanish, *c*.1900. *Private collection.*

100 Tin-glazed tile with hand-stencilled in-glaze decoration depicting a central diagonal floral display. Quarter design borders. Pink, blue and orange. Plastic clay, 203 x 203mm. Spanish, *c*.1900. *Private collection.*

101–112 Group of Dutch tin-glazed tiles with hand-painted and stencilled in-glaze decoration of flowers, river scenes, repeat designs and stylized flower motifs. Blue, red, yellow, green and purple.
Plastic clay, each tile 150 x 150mm.
Made by firms such as Van Hulst, Harlingen, and Ravesteijn, Utrecht, in the late 19th century. Made for the British market with a 6in format to comply with British measurements.
Private collection.

113–118 Group of French tin-glazed tiles with hand-stencilled in-glaze decoration of stylized motifs, repeat patterns and borders. Blue with some purple.
Plastic clay, each tile 110 x 110mm.
Made in small factories around Beauvais (Oise) during the 19th century by firms such as Ledoux at Ponchon. Most stamped with the makers' names.
Private collection.

119 Two French tin-glazed tiles with hand-painted in-glaze decoration depicting country women within a quatrefoil against a trellis of flower-heads. Purple.
Plastic clay, each tile 127 x 127mm.
Made in Desvres, Pas-de-Calais, northern France, 1850–1900.
Private collection.

120–122 *See 124–126.*

123 Four French tin-glazed tiles with hand-painted in-glaze decoration of a design based on a quadrant with daisies and tulips. Yellow, blue, green and purple.
Plastic clay, each tile 130 x 130mm.
Made by Fourmaintraux, Desvres, Pas-de-Calais, northern France, 1850–1900.
Private collection.

120–122 and 124–126 Groups of French tin-glazed tiles with stencilled in-glaze decoration of geometric motifs and patterns. Blue, yellow and purple.
Plastic clay, each tile 110 x 110mm.
Made in Desvres, Pas-de-Calais, northern France by such manufacturers as Fourmaintraux, 1850–1900.
Private collection.

127 Four Dutch tiles with hand-painted in-glaze decoration of a central star motif, surrounded by pomegranates, tulips and grapes. Blue.
Plastic clay, each tile 130 x 130mm.
Early-17th century.
Private collection.

128 German stove tile, relief-moulded and modelled design of a horseman of Kurfurst, Brandenburg, and figures of the four seasons. Green.
Plastic clay, 500 x 270mm.
Nuremburg, 16th century.
City Museum & Art Gallery, Stoke-on-Trent.

129 Tin-glazed panel of 12 tiles with hand-painted in-glaze decoration depicting a St Rosalina nun holding a lily and an open book. Orange, blue and green.
Plastic clay, each tile 128 x 128mm.
Italian, 18th century.
Glasgow City Museums & Art Galleries.

GOTHIC REVIVAL TILES

130 Four glazed encaustic floor tiles. Floreated design based on medieval original at Great Malvern, Worcestershire.
Plastic clay, each tile 150 x 150mm.
Chamberlain, early-1840s.
Private collection.

131 Four glazed encaustic border tiles. Medieval design with birds and foliage.
Plastic clay, each tile 127 x 152mm.
Minton & Co, *c.*1890.
Private collection.

132 Unglazed encaustic floor tile with an inlaid design of stylized leaves within a quatrefoil with fleur-de-lis corner motifs. Based on a design by A W N Pugin.
Plastic clay, 150 x 150mm.
Minton & Co, *c.*1850.
Private collection.

133 Unglazed encaustic floor tile with an inlaid design of a fleur-de-lis. Plastic clay, 150 x 150mm. Minton & Co, c.1850. *Private collection.*

134 Unglazed encaustic floor tile with an inlaid design of a fleur-de-lis. Based on a design by A W N Pugin. Plastic clay, 150 x 150mm. Minton & Co, c.1850. *Private collection.*

135–138 Four line-impressed tiles with translucent glazes and medieval style designs. Plastic clay, each tile 108 x 108mm. Craven Dunnill, c.1880. *Private collection.*

139 Nine unglazed encaustic floor tiles with the inlaid design overpainted with yellow glaze, medieval style design. Plastic clay, each tile 147 x 147mm. Minton & Co, c.1860. *City Museum & Art Gallery, Stoke-on-Trent.*

140 Unglazed encaustic floor tile with a representation of a lion. Designed by A W N Pugin for the Palace of Westminster. Plastic clay, 150 x 150mm. Minton & Co, c.1850. *Private collection.*

141 Unglazed encaustic floor tile with a yellow-glazed Knight Templar on horseback. Plastic clay, 150 x 150mm. Minton & Co, c.1842. *Private collection.*

142 Glazed encaustic floor tile with a rampant lion, coat of arms of the Talbot family, Earls of Shrewsbury. Plastic clay, 150 x 150mm. Minton & Co, date mark for 1868. *Private collection.*

143 Unglazed encaustic floor tile with inscription, 'DOMINI IN SANGUINE TUO', around a Tudor Rose. Designed by A W N Pugin for St Augustine's Church, Ramsgate. Plastic clay, 150 x 150mm. Minton & Co, c.1850. *Tiles & Architectural Ceramics Society.*

144 Unglazed encaustic floor tile with buff inlaid parts. Plastic clay, 150 x 150mm. Minton & Co, c.1850. *Private collection.*

145–146 Two unglazed encaustic floor tiles with buff inlaid parts overpainted with yellow glaze. Fleurs-de-lis motifs within quadrants. Designed by A W N Pugin. Plastic clay, each tile 150 x 150mm. Minton & Co, c.1850. *Tiles & Architectural Ceramics Society.*

147 Glazed encaustic tile of a fleur-de-lis. Dust-pressed, 105 x 105mm. Godwin, c.1865. *Private collection.*

148–149 Two glazed inlaid tiles with fleurs-de-lis designs, illustrating the dependence of the 19th century designer on medieval originals. The tile on the left (No 148) is from a 14th century Nottingham kiln. Plastic clay, 52 x 52mm. The tile on the right (No 149) is a Gothic Revival tile of the 1870s. *Private collection.*

150 Five glazed encaustic floor tiles with dimpled surfaces imitating a 'medieval' look. Designed by A W N Pugin. Plastic clay, central tile 150 x 150mm. Minton & Co, c.1895. *Private collection.*

151 Panel of five unglazed encaustic floor tiles. Circular central tile shows the Holy Lamb set within Gothic Revival style motifs designed by A W N Pugin. Plastic clay, panel measures 580 x 580mm. Minton & Co, late-1840s onward. *Private collection.*

152 Panel of 16 glazed encaustic floor tiles with medieval-style motifs. Dust-pressed, each tile 110 x 110mm. Godwin, c.1870. *Private collection.*

153 Panel of four glazed majolica tiles from the large free-standing stove in the Medieval Court of the Great Exhibition.
Plastic clay, each tile 250 x 250mm.
Minton & Co, 1851.
The original watercolour sketches for these tiles, signed by A W N Pugin, are preserved at the Minton Museum library, Royal Doulton Tableware, Stoke-on-Trent.
Private collection.

154 Panel of 25 glazed majolica wall tiles. Gothic Revival style motifs based on flowers and foliage.
Dust-pressed, each tile 150 x 150mm.
Campbell Brick & Tile Co, 1873.
Originally lined the walls of the apse of Christ Church, Scarborough (demolished 1979).
Private collection.

155 Panel of 25 glazed majolica wall tiles with added gold leaf. Gothic Revival style motifs with a central design of the Holy Lamb carrying the banner of St George and the symbols of the four evangelists in the outer corners.
Dust-pressed, each tile 150 x 150mm.
Campbell Brick & Tile Co, 1873.
Originally part of the altar reredos of Christ Church, Scarborough (demolished 1979).
Private collection.

156 Tile with a moulded relief design of two birds painted with majolica glazes.
Dust-pressed.
Minton, Hollins & Co, *c*.1860.
Private collection.

157 Unglazed encaustic floor tile depicting an eagle with a spear.
Plastic clay, 150 x 150mm.
Minton & Co, *c*.1860.
Jackfield Tile Museum.

158 Unglazed encaustic floor tile with the letters 'ABKR' within a circular motif.
Plastic clay, 150 x 150mm.
Minton & Co, *c*.1860.
Jackfield Tile Museum.

159 Block-printed tile in blue on a white ground.
Dust-pressed, 205 x 205mm.
Minton's China Works, *c*.1875.
This design also appears in A W N Pugin's *Floreated Ornament*, 1849.
Private collection.

160 Glazed majolica tile depicting the Holy Lamb designed by E W Pugin (son of A W N Pugin).
Dust-pressed, 330 x 330mm.
Craven Dunnill, *c*.1875.
Private collection.

161 Tile with under-glaze transfer-printed and hand-painted decoration depicting the Holy IHS monogram emblazoned on a star.
Dust-pressed, 152 x 152mm.
T & R Boote, Burslem, early-20th century.
City Museum & Art Gallery, Stoke-on-Trent.

162 Unglazed encaustic tile, heraldic shield with coat of arms of Earl Lovelace.
Plastic clay, 300 x 300mm.
Minton & Co, *c*.1865.
Private collection.

163 Tile with block-printed over-glaze decoration with a Gothic Revival motif designed by A W N Pugin.
Dust-pressed, 233 x 233mm.
Minton & Co, *c*.1850.
City Museum & Art Gallery, Stoke-on-Trent.

164 Glazed encaustic tile with a memorial inscription for Robert Thorpe (died 1872).
Plastic clay, 300 x 300mm.
Minton & Co, 1872.
Jackfield Tile Museum.

MINTON TILES

165 Four under-glaze block-printed tiles depicting the four seasons. Designed by John Moyr Smith. Dust-pressed, each tile 150 x 150mm. Minton's China Works, *c*.1875.
Private collection.

166 Tile with under-glaze printed decoration from an early series by Minton called *Watteau* subjects. Dust-pressed (with Prosser's Patent credited on the reverse), 150 x 150mm. Minton & Co, *c*.1845.
Private collection.

167 Tile with under-glaze printed decoration of a sunflower within a border of other plants and flowers. Dust-pressed, 150 x 150mm. Minton's China Works, *c*.1880.
Glasgow Museums & Art Galleries.

168 Tile with under-glaze printed decoration. From a series of ten birds. Dust-pressed, 150 x 150mm. Minton, Hollins & Co, *c*.1875.
Private collection.

169 Tile with under-glaze hand-painted decoration of birds. From a wildlife series. Dust-pressed, 150 x 150mm. Minton, Hollins & Co, *c*.1875.
Private collection.

170–171 Two tiles with under-glaze printed decoration with two Classical female heads.
From a series of eight.
Dust-pressed, each tile 150 x 150mm. Minton, Hollins & Co, *c*.1875.
Private collection.

172 Tile with under-glaze printed decoration depicting the Willow Pattern.
Dust-pressed, 150 x 150mm. Minton's China Works, *c*.1880.
Private collection.

173 Tile with under-glaze printed decoration of an oriental design.
Dust-pressed, 150 x 150mm. Minton's China Works, *c*.1880.
Private collection.

174 Four under-glaze printed tiles depicting rural activities associated with the four seasons.
Dust-pressed, 150 x 150mm. Minton, Hollins & Co, *c*.1875.
Private collection.

175 Four tiles with under-glaze printed decoration depicting four scenes.
Designed by William Wise.
Dust-pressed, each tile 150 x 150mm. Minton's China Works, *c*.1880.
Private collection.

176 Tile with a hand-painted landscape. Designed by E J Poynter, 260 x 260mm. Produced at Minton's Art Pottery Studio, Kensington Gore, London, 1868. Similar tiles are in the Grill Room of the Victoria and Albert Museum.
Private collection.

177 Tile with under-glaze printed decoration of an oriental landscape with a pagoda set within a circle. Dust-pressed, 150 x 150mm. Minton, Hollins & Co, *c*.1875.
Private collection.

178 Black tile, partly glazed. Unglazed horse motif in relief in the centre within a gold star with square corners. Dust-pressed, 150 x 150mm. Minton, *c*.1870.
Private collection.

179 Tile with under-glaze printed decoration depicting a scene with two lovers. From the *Albert Durer* series representing medieval German life. Dust-pressed, 204 x 204mm. Minton's China Works, *c*.1880.
Private collection.

180 Tile with under-glaze printed decoration of a continental townscape. Dust-pressed, 205 x 205mm. Minton's China Works, *c*.1880.
Private collection.

181 Tile with on-glaze photo-chromolithograph representing a Classical scene depicting *Jupiter and Calista*.
Based on a painting by Angelica Kaufmann.
Dust-pressed, 205 x 205mm.
Minton, Hollins & Co, *c*.1870.
Private collection.

182 Tile with under-glaze hand-painted decoration depicting children dressed in costumes representing *The Labours of the Months*.
Designed by Stacey Marks and painted by Mrs C Keats.
Plastic clay, 200 x 410mm.
Minton's Art Pottery Studio, Kensington Gore, London *c*.1873.
Private collection.

183–184 Two tiles with under-glaze printed decoration with scenes depicting *And Let Me The Canakin Clink* and *Blow Thou Winter Wind*.
From the series of 12 tiles of *Shakespearean Songs*.
Designed by John Moyr Smith.
Dust-pressed, each tile 205 x 205mm.
Minton, Hollins & Co, *c*.1880.
Glasgow Museums and Art Galleries and private collection.

185–186 Two tiles with printed designs and hand-added colour of medieval life.
Designed by Stacey Marks. From his series *The Seven Ages of Man*.
Plastic clay, 230 x 230mm.
Minton's Art Pottery Studio, Kensington Gore, London,*c*.1873.
Private collection.

187 Tile with an over-glaze hand-painted scene of *The Dutiful Grandson*.
Dust-pressed, 204 x 204mm.
Minton's China Works, *c*.1875.
Private collection.

188 Tile with Japanese-style decoration with gold over-painting.
Dust-pressed, 203 x 203mm.
Minton's China Works, *c*.1880.
Private collection.

189 Set of 12 under-glaze printed tiles depicting *Aesop's Fables*.
Designed by John Moyr Smith.
Dust-pressed, each tile 150 x 150mm.
Minton's China Works, *c*.1875.
Private collection.

190 Tile with under-glaze hand-painted decoration of a reclining woman in Classical robes, inscribed 'MORNING'.
Dust-pressed, 205 x 205mm.
Painted on a Minton, Hollins & Co blank, *c*.1880.
Private collection.

191 Panel of 16 majolica tiles.
Dust-pressed, each tile 150 x 150mm.
Minton, Hollins & Co, *c*.1870.
Private collection.

192–199 Eight tiles with majolica glazes with various designs.
Dust-pressed, each tile 150 x 150mm, except No 195.
Minton, Hollins & Co and Minton's China Works, 1870–1900.
Private collection.

200 Tile with a relief design covered with a single translucent glaze, depicting the personification of Spring.
Dust-pressed, 203 x 203mm.
Minton, Hollins & Co, 1875.
Private collection.

201 Panel of three tiles decorated with coloured opaque slip under a clear glaze depicting a heron in a pond.
Dust-pressed, each tile 150 x 150mm.
Attributed to Minton, Hollins & Co, *c*.1870.
Private collection.

202 Glazed encaustic floor tile, inlaid design of lily of the valley within a Gothic Revival style border.
Plastic clay, 150 x 150mm.
Minton & Co, *c*.1870.
Private collection.

203 Unglazed encaustic floor tile with a monogram of the letters 'O' and 'H'.
Plastic clay, 150 x 150mm.
Minton & Co, *c.*1863.
Private collection.

204 Unglazed encaustic circular tile with the head of Medusa.
Plastic clay, 910mm diameter.
Minton & Co, 1895.
The centre-piece of a large floor ordered by the American millionaire Mr Astor for his residence at Clevedon, Buckinghamshire.
Private collection.

205 Tile with a relief design with a single translucent glaze depicting a dancing girl in diaphanous robes.
Plastic clay, 155 x 475mm.
Minton, Hollins & Co, *c.*1870.
Private collection.

206 Tile with under-glaze printed decoration based on a hand-painted Dutch tile pattern.
Dust-pressed, 203 x 203mm.
Minton, Hollins & Co, *c.*1875.
Private collection.

207 Panel of nine unglazed encaustic tiles with stylized Classical motifs.
Plastic clay, central tile 150 x 150mm.
Minton & Co, *c.*1865.
Private collection.

208 Unglazed encaustic floor tile with a Classical motif.
Plastic clay, 150 x 150mm.
Minton & Co, *c.*1865.
Private collection.

209 Unglazed encaustic floor tile with a Roman design.
Plastic clay, 150 x 150mm.
Minton & Co, *c.*1865.
Private collection.

210 Three tiles with on-glaze hand-painted decoration of *Lebanon Cedar Cones*, *Horse Chestnut Blossom* and *Horse Chestnut Conkers*. Painted by Miss Ada Hanbury for the 1878 Paris Exhibition.
Dust-pressed, each approx. 200 x 200mm.
Minton's China Works, *c.*1875.
Private collection.

211 Set of 12 under-glaze printed tiles with scenes from Scott's *Waverley* novels. Designed by John Moyr Smith.
Dust-pressed, each tile 204 x 204mm.
Minton's China Works, *c.*1875.
Private collection.

212 Panel of 64 unglazed encaustic floor tiles with a central Classical motif. Greek palmette corners.
Plastic clay, square tiles 150 x 150mm.
Minton & Co, *c.*1865.
City Museum & Art Gallery, Stoke-on-Trent.

MAW TILES

213 Three unglazed encaustic tiles with white letters 'M', 'A', 'W' on blue.
Plastic clay, 108 x 108mm.
Maw & Co, *c.*1865.
Jackfield Tile Museum.

214 Unglazed patent mosaic floor tile with continuous scroll design in white and brown on orange.
Dust-pressed, 150 x 150mm.
Maw & Co, *c.*1870.
Jackfield Tile Museum.

215 Four unglazed encaustic floor tiles forming a repeat circular foliate pattern. in green, white, blue, buff and red.
Plastic clay, 150 x 150mm.
Maw & Co, *c.*1860.
Jackfield Tile Museum.

216 Partially enamelled red terracotta tile with relief decoration of flowers.
Dust-pressed, 150 x 150mm.
Maw & Co, *c.*1880.
Private collection.

217 Fireplace tile, transfer-printed and hand-painted, depicting a mallard drake with wings extended.
Maw catalogue No. 2198.
Dust-pressed, 405 x 230mm.
Maw & Co, *c.*1870.
Private collection.

218 Glazed 'Anglo-Persian' tile with transfer-printed and hand-painted design of Persian-style flowers and foliage in blue, turquoise and green on white.
Plastic clay, 200 x 200mm.
Maw & Co, *c*.1880.
Private collection.

219 Brown glazed, relief-decorated tile.
Dust-pressed, 150 x 26mm.
Maw & Co, *c*.1870.
Jackfield Tile Museum.

220 Glazed majolica tile of interlocking lozenges filled with Moorish motifs.
Dust-pressed, 150 x 37mm.
Maw & Co, *c*.1860.
Jackfield Tile Museum.

221 Relief-decorated *pâte-sur-pâte* tile of a crested bird on a branch in white against brown. Part of a fireplace panel.
Dust-pressed, 150 x 150mm.
Maw & Co, *c*.1865.
Private collection.

222 Unglazed encaustic trade tile with buff lettering on red: 'THIS TILE MANUFACTURED BY MAW & CO, SHROPSHIRE, ENGLAND. IMPORTED AND LAID BY THE HENRY DIBBLEE CO, CHICAGO, ILLS, USA '.
Plastic clay, 150 x 150mm.
Maw & Co, *c*.1860.
Jackfield Tile Museum.

223 Glazed, barbotine-painted tile decorated with sprays of red and yellow chrysanthemums.
Dust-pressed, 304 x 152 mm.
Maw & Co, *c*.1880.
Private collection.

224 Partially enamelled red terracotta tile with high relief scallop shell design.
Dust-pressed, 150 x 150mm.
Maw & Co, *c*.1880.
Private collection.

225 Glazed block-printed tile decorated with naturalistic honeysuckle.
Dust-pressed, 200 x 200mm.
Maw & Co, *c*.1880.
Gladstone Pottery Museum.

226 Six glazed tiles printed and hand-painted in sepia, depicting two female figures in Classical dress.
Dust-pressed, 150 x 150mm.
Maw & Co, 1883.
Part of the original scheme for the entrance hall and staircase at Maw & Co's factory, Jackfield.
Jackfield Tile Museum.

227 Glazed tile with printed decoration in blue on white of a Japanese lady.
Designed by Owen Gibbons.
Dust-pressed, 150 x 300mm.
Maw & Co, *c*.1885. [*See also* No 423.]
Jackfield Tile Museum.

228 Two glazed tiles with hand-painted lustre foliage and flowers in red and gold.
Dust-pressed, each tile 150 x 150mm.
Maw & Co, *c*.1880.
Private collection.

229 Glazed tile with hand-painted design of a spider's web among branches.
Dust-pressed, 150 x 150mm.
Maw & Co, *c*.1880.
Private collection.

230 Three glazed tiles with hand-painted flowers and foliage in ruby lustre.
Dust-pressed, each tile 150 x 150mm.
Maw & Co, *c*.1880.
Private collection.

231 Glazed tile block-printed in brown on cream with design of *The Pharisee and Publican*.
Designed by C O Murray as part of *The Parables of the New Testament* series.
Dust-pressed, 205 x 205mm.
Maw & Co, *c*.1880.
Private collection.

232 Glazed tile, block-printed in sepia on cream with design of *The Lost Piece of Silver* by C O Murray as part of *The Parables of the New Testament* series.
Dust-pressed, 205 x 205mm.
Maw & Co, *c*.1880.
Private collection.

233 Glazed tile in a metal frame forming a teapot stand, decorated with a highly stylized flower and leaves in yellow and lustre.
Dust-pressed, 150 x 150mm.
Maw & Co, *c*.1900.
Jackfield Tile Museum.

234 Glazed tile with a printed and hand-painted geometric design.
Dust-pressed, 105 x 105mm.
Maw & Co, *c*.1885.
Gladstone Pottery Museum.

235 Hand-painted, red lustre glazed tile with stylized paeony.
Design attributed to Lewis F Day.
Dust-pressed, 152 x 151mm.
J C Edwards, Ruabon, North Wales, *c*.1880.
Private collection.

236 Panel of glazed majolica tiles with relief decoration. Dado arrangement of diagonally-placed tiles with stylized floral motifs separated by strips. Frieze above with stylized peacocks and flowers. Maroon, buff, brown, green and pale blue.
Designed for the 1867 Paris Exhibition.
Dust-pressed, various sizes.
Maw & Co, 1867.
Private collection.

237 High relief-decorated tile glazed in brown with oak leaf and acorn design.
Dust-pressed, 150 x 150mm.
Maw & Co, *c*.1880.
Private collection.

238 Four glazed tiles with relief design in pink, green, brown and black on white.
Dust-pressed, each tile 150 x 150mm.
Maw & Co, *c*.1870.
Private collection.

CRAVEN DUNNILL TILES

239 Two block-printed glazed frieze tiles with a design of fish and weeds in dark blue on white.
Dust-pressed, each tile 150 x 150mm.
Craven Dunnill & Co, *c*.1890.
Jackfield Tile Museum.

240 Glazed relief-decorated tile of a monk holding a candle in a cellar in green.
Dust-pressed, 300 x 150mm.
Craven Dunnill & Co, *c*.1890.
Jackfield Tile Museum.

241 Unglazed encaustic trade tile with buff lettering on red 'CRAVEN DUNNILL'S JACKFIELD MOSAIC'.
Plastic clay, 150 x 70mm.
Craven Dunnill & Co, *c*.1880.
Jackfield Tile Museum.

242 Hand-painted tile with a stylized blue flower and green foliage between maroon and lilac bands.
Dust-pressed, 150 x 75mm.
Craven Dunnill & Co, *c*.1890.
Jackfield Tile Museum.

243 Glazed tile with printed and hand-painted decoration of a flower with leaves.
Plastic clay, 150 x 150mm.
Craven Dunnill & Co, *c*.1880.
Private collection.

244 Six patent mosaic floor tiles of irregular shape with the *tesserae* in a fan layout.
Dust-pressed, various sizes.
Craven Dunnill & Co, *c*.1880.
Private collection.

245 Glazed block-printed tile with a female face flanked by stylized birds in buff on brown.
Dust-pressed, 200 x 200mm.
Craven Dunnill & Co, *c*.1890.
Private collection.

246 Glazed tile with stencilled and hand-painted lustre decoration with a floral design.
Dust-pressed, 150 x 150mm.
Craven Dunnill & Co, *c*.1880.
Private collection.

247 Glazed tile with stencilled and hand-painted lustre decoration with a floral design.
Dust-pressed, 150 x 150mm.
Craven Dunnill & Co, *c.*1880.
Private collection.

248 Glazed encaustic floor tile with a medieval-style design in brown and black sparkle.
Plastic clay, 150 x 150mm.
Craven Dunnill & Co, *c.*1875.
Jackfield Tile Museum.

249 Ruby lustre hand-painted tile with a lion design.
Dust-pressed, 150 x 150mm.
Craven Dunnill & Co, *c.*1890.
Jackfield Tile Museum.

250 Eight glazed wall tiles decorated with scrolling foliage in red lustre and yellow.
Dust-pressed, each tile 150 x 150mm.
Craven Dunnill & Co, *c.*1900.
From the tiled dado of a public house in Balham, London.
Jackfield Tile Museum.

WEDGWOOD TILES

251 Tile with transfer-printed outline and hand-coloured under-glaze 'Persian' design on a green body. Green, blue, orange, red and white colouring.
Dust-pressed, 200 x 200mm.
Wedgwood, *c.*1885.
City Museum & Art Gallery, Stoke-on-Trent.

252 Tile with Marsden patent 'impressed' decoration (stencilled slip). Spray of flowers and leaves.
Dust-pressed, 150 x 150mm.
Wedgwood, *c.*1890.
Private collection.

253 Tile with Marsden patent 'impressed' decoration (stencilled slip). Sprays of blossom and leaves in white, brown and green slips on grey-green body under a clear glaze.
Dust-pressed, 152 x 152mm.
Wedgwood, *c.*1885.
Private collection.

254 Tile with Marsden patent 'impressed' decoration (stencilled slip). Blossom and foliage design in blue, white and yellow slips on green body under a clear glaze.
Dust-pressed, 152 x 152mm.
Wedgwood, *c.*1885.
Private collection.

255 Tile with Marsden patent 'impressed' decoration (stencilled slip). Spray of flowers and leaves.
Dust-pressed, 150 x 150mm.
Wedgwood, *c.*1890.
Private collection.

256 Tile with a transfer-printed design of a dog's head in blue on white under a clear glaze.
Designed by H Hope-Crealock.
Dust-pressed, 152 x 152mm.
Wedgwood, *c.*1885.
Private collection.

257 Set of 12 tiles with transfer-printed designs of characters from Shakespeare's *A Midsummer Night's Dream*. Brown on cream body under a clear glaze.
Designed by Helen J A Miles and signed on each tile in the print.
Dust-pressed, each tile 150 x 150mm.
Wedgwood, *c.*1882.
Private collection.

258 Four tiles from a set of 12. Transfer-printed in under-glaze blue-on-white with scenes of children depicting the months of the year, entitled *Old English*.
Designed by Helen J A Miles.
Dust-pressed, each tile 152 x 152mm.
Wedgwood, *c.*1890.
Private collection.

DOULTON TILES

259 Tile with Marsden patent 'impressed' decoration (stencilled slip) on a lace-textured background (Slater's patent) with additional hand-painting and gold decoration, clear glazed.
Dust-pressed, 150 x 150mm.
Doulton & Co, Lambeth, *c.*1895.
Private collection.

260 Four tiles, hand-painted underglaze in browns, blues, greens and yellows, depicting female figures symbolic of the four seasons.
Dust-pressed, 152 x 152mm.
Doulton & Co, Lambeth, *c.*1880.
Private collection.

261 Two tiles with tube-lined designs of floral motifs.
Dust-pressed, 150 x 150mm.
Decorated by Doulton & Co, Lambeth, on Minton, Hollins & Co blanks, *c.*1885.
Private collection.

262 Two tiles, sgraffito decorated with an equestrian scene. Design incised into off-white slip with a blue stain rubbed in. Designed and executed by Hannah Barlow.
Plastic clay, each tile 200 x 200mm.
Doulton & Co, Lambeth, *c.*1880.
Private collection.

263–264 Two tiles with transfer-printed and hand-coloured views of Chatham (No 263) and Wouldham (No 264) in yellow, brown, mauve and green. From a series of places in Kent mentioned in the Domesday Book. Designed by Donald Maxwell. Signed 'DM'.
Dust-pressed, each tile 140 x 165mm.
Doulton & Co, Woolliscroft blanks, 1935.
Private collection.

265 Four tiles, hand-painted with an Aesthetic Movement design of a vase of blossom and rushes in blues, greens, brown and yellow on a cream ground.
Dust-pressed, three tiles 200 x 200mm, bottom tile 200 x 100mm.
Doulton & Co, Lambeth, on Minton, Hollins & Co blanks, *c.*1880.
Private collection.

PILKINGTON TILES AND MARTIN BROTHERS TILES

266–267 Two tiles with designs of monastic scenes under an olive glaze. Designed by Joseph Kwiatkowski (signed).
Dust-pressed, each tile 305 x 152mm.
Pilkington, *c.*1900.
Private collection.

268 Tile with a moulded design of a floral spray under green, blue and cream translucent glazes.
Designed by Lewis F Day.
Dust-pressed, 304 x 152mm.
Pilkington, *c.*1905.
Private collection.

269 Tile with hand-painted underglaze decoration of a sailing ship.
Plastic clay, 78 x 78mm.
Pilkington, *c.*1900.
Private collection.

270 Tile, moulded with a stylized galley under turquoise, brown, cream and pink glazes.
Dust-pressed, 155 x 155mm.
Pilkington, *c.*1905.
Private collection.

271 Tile moulded with a stylized sailing ship under turquoise, brown and fawn glazes.
Dust-pressed, 155 x 155mm.
Pilkington, *c.*1905.
Private collection.

272 Tile with a tube-lined design of a ship in blues, browns and green glazes Designed and executed by Edmund Kent.
Dust-pressed, 304 x 152mm.
Pilkington, *c.*1910.
Private collection.

273 Tile with a tube-lined galleon in brown, orang, greens, blue and fawn. Designed and executed by Edmund Kent. Dust-pressed, 305 x 152mm. Pilkington, *c.*1910. *Private collection.*

274 Salt-glazed stoneware tile moulded with a design of seaweed in blue and grey. Plastic clay, 152 x 152mm. Martin Brothers, Southall, *c.*1875. *Private collection.*

275 Salt-glazed stoneware tile with an incised design of foliage and poppy heads in brown and grey, partly lustred. Plastic clay, 152 x 152mm. Martin Brothers, Southall, *c.*1895. *Private collection.*

276 Four tiles, hand-painted with a Persian design of stylized flowers in blues, greens and orange. Plastic clay, each tile 152 x 152mm. Pilkington, *c.*1905. *Private collection.*

277 Panel of 24 tiles, hand-painted with a scene of people dancing around a maypole in green, brown, yellow and blue Dust-pressed, each tile 152 x 152mm. Pilkington, *c.*1920. Originally used at branches of Maypole Dairies. *Private collection.*

BURMANTOFTS TILES

278 Large moulded plaque depicting a female figure in flowing robes inscribed 'ROME'. Buff earthenware with white slip under a translucent olive glaze. Plastic clay, 920 x 460mm. Burmantofts, *c.*1890. *Leeds City Museums.*

279 Moulded plaque depicting a diaphanously clad Classical female figure. Buff earthenware with white slip under a translucent orange-yellow glaze. Plastic clay, 930 x 225mm. Burmantofts, *c.*1890. *Leeds City Museums.*

280 Moulded plaque depicting a female figure holding a sheaf of corn symbolic of summer. Yellow-green and turquoise glazes. Plastic clay, 620 x 225mm. Burmantofts, *c.*1895. *Leeds City Museums.*

281 Panel of ten tiles, barbotine painted with a design of lilies in blues, greens and browns on a white ground under a clear glaze. Dust-pressed, each tile 152 x 152mm. Burmantofts, *c.*1905. *Leeds City Museums.*

282 Moulded tile with a Bacchanalian scene under a light purplish-brown glaze. Plastic clay, 124 x 163mm. Burmantofts, *c.*1882. *Leeds City Museums.*

283 Moulded tile with a bird and flowers under a blue glaze. Plastic clay, 155 x 155mm. Burmantofts, *c.*1880. *Leeds City Museums.*

284 Moulded tile with chicks sheltering under a leaf, olive green glaze. Plastic clay, 230 x 230mm. Burmantofts, *c.*1890. *Private collection.*

285 Set of 11 moulded tiles depicting animals and foliage with various dark-coloured glazes. Plastic clay, 100 x 100mm. Burmantofts, *c.*1890. *Private collection.*

286 Panel of ten tiles tube-lined with a Viking long-boat in a cartouche surrounded by stylized Art Nouveau flowers in green, olive, yellow, red and blue glazes. Plastic clay, each tile 152 x 152mm. Burmantofts, *c.*1905. *Leeds City Museums.*

287 Moulded tile with a man and a woman at a table writing a letter, under an olive-green glaze, entitled *The Letterwriters*.
Designed by Joseph Kwiatkowski (signed).
Plastic clay, 200 x 300mm.
Pilkington, *c*.1905. Often mis-attributed to Burmantofts. [*See also* Nos 266 & 267.]
Leeds City Museums.

288 Glazed trade tile of the Leeds Fireclay Co Ltd, Wortley, Leeds.
Plastic clay, 170 x 140mm, *c*.1900.
Leeds City Museums.

289 Border tile with Classical relief-moulded design covered with a translucent glaze.
Dust-pressed, 150 x 75mm.
Burmantofts, *c*.1890.
Leeds City Museums.

290 Tile with relief-moulded decoration of two gryphons under coloured glazes.
Plastic clay, 300 x 150mm.
Burmantofts, *c*.1885.
Leeds City Museums.

291 Tile with relief-moulded design under coloured glazes with a spray of three flowers.
Plastic clay, 200 x 150mm.
Burmantofts, *c*.1885.
Leeds City Museums.

292 Tile with relief-moulded decoration with coloured glazes of a Classical spiral design of a stem with a flower.
Plastic clay, 200 x 200mm.
Burmantofts, *c*.1885.
Leeds City Museums.

293–294 Two tiles with flowers barbotine painted in coloured slip and covered with a transparent glaze.
Plastic clay, each tile 400 x 200mm.
Burmantofts, *c*.1885.
Leeds City Museums.

SIMPSON TILES

295 Tile with under-glaze hand-painted decoration of a swallow in flight.
Plastic clay, 150 x 150mm.
W B Simpson & Sons, *c*.1875.
Private collection.

296 Three tiles with under-glaze hand-painted decoration of fish among weed.
Dust-pressed, each tile 150 x 150mm.
W B Simpson & Sons, *c*.1880.
Private collection.

297 Three tiles with hand-painted under-glaze decoration of seaweed and shells.
Dust-pressed, each tile 151 x 126mm.
W B Simpson & Sons, *c*.1880.
Private collection.

298 Two tiles with under-glaze decoration of foliage.
Dust-pressed, each tile 150 x 150mm.
W B Simpson & Sons, *c*.1880.
Private collection.

299 Four under-glaze hand-painted tiles with representations of the four seasons.
Plastic clay, 152 x 152mm.
W B Simpson & Sons, *c*.1875.
Private collection.

300 Tile with under-glaze hand-painted decoration depicting fruit in a roundel.
Dust-pressed, 202 x 202mm.
W B Simpson & Sons, *c*.1875.
Private collection.

301 Tile with machine-pressed relief decoration with translucent glazes depicting a spray of lilac blossom in a roundel.
Dust-pressed, 150 x 150mm.
T A Simpson & Co, *c*.1890.
Private collection.

302 Tile with under-glaze hand-painted decoration representing Ceres, the Roman goddess of tillage and corn.
Plastic clay, 615 x 205mm.
W B Simpson & Sons, *c*.1875.
Private collection.

COPELAND TILES

303 Tile with printed and hand-painted under-glaze decoration of a scene from Shakespeare's *Merchant of Venice*.
Plastic clay, 200 x 200mm.
Copeland, *c*.1875.
Private collection.

304–305 Two tiles with printed and hand-painted under-glaze decoration with scenes from Shakespeare's *Macbeth* and *Henry IV*, *Part 1*.
Plastic clay, each tile 150 x 150mm.
Copeland, *c*.1875.
Private collection.

306–307 Two tiles with printed and hand-painted under-glaze decoration with scenes of gnomes and elves.
From a series of 12 subjects.
Plastic clay, each tile 150 x 150mm.
Copeland, *c*.1875.
Private collection.

308 Tile with dry-cord technique decoration (*cuerda seca*) of a floral design.
Plastic clay, 152 x 152mm.
Copeland, *c*.1880.
Private collection.

309 Tile with relief decoration of *Earth*.
Plastic clay, 203 x 203mm.
Copeland, 1877.
Private collection.

310 Curved tile with printed and hand-coloured over-glaze decoration with a floral spray.
Plastic clay, 198 x 18 x 145mm.
Copeland and Garrett, *c*.1835.
Private collection.

311 Tile with under-glaze transfer-printed decoration representing a scene entitled *A Patriot at Sea*.
Plastic clay, 150 x 150mm.
Possibly Spode or Copeland, *c*.1825.
Private collection.

312 Tile with printed and hand-painted under-glaze decoration of a minstrel.
Plastic clay, 150 x 150mm.
Copeland, 1878.
Private collection.

313 Large plaque with hand-painted on-glaze decoration and raised gold paste of two figures in a landscape with a waterfall in the tradition of Watteau. Set in a gold trellis and floral border.
Plastic clay, 900 x 200mm.
Copeland & Garrett, *c*.1835.
Private collection.

314 Tile with hand-painted decoration depicting a Chinese scene with a bird and blossom tree.
Plastic clay, 200 x 200mm.
Copeland & Garrett, *c*.1835.
Private collection.

315 Three tiles with printed and hand-painted under-glaze decoration depicting minstrels set against an on-glaze gold background.
Copeland, *c*.1875.
Private collection.

OTHER TILEMAKERS

316 Tile with incised picture of a girl reading a book. Salt-glazed stoneware with some blue and olive colouring.
Designed by C Kettle, 200 x 250mm.
Cox & Sons, Fulham, London, *c*.1875.
Private collection.

317 Tile with a moulded design of fish swimming amongst weeds, with the design further undercut by hand, olive glaze.
Dust-pressed, 152 x 152mm.
Marsden Tile Co, *c*.1895.
Private collection.

318 Tile with oriental scene of wading birds in raised gold and silver paste on a matt black ground with hand-painted on-glaze border decoration executed by Humi, a Japanese artist at Minton's China Works.
Dust-pressed, 204 x 44mm.
Minton's China Works, *c*.1880.
Private collection.

319 Tile set in a teapot stand, decorated with dry-cord technique (*cuerda seca*) depicting a Persian-style design.
Dust-pressed, 204 x 204mm.
Decorated by A Wenger (glaze makers) on a George Woolliscroft blank, *c.*1900.
Gladstone Pottery Museum.

320 Tile with a slip-trailed design commemorating Queen Victoria's Golden Jubilee, 1887.
Dust-pressed, 152 x 152mm.
J C Edwards, Ruabon, North Wales, 1887.
Private collection.

321 Tile with a floral design in barbotine and sgraffito technique under a transparent glaze.
Dust-pressed, 300 x 150mm.
Flaxman (J & W Wade), *c.*1890.
Private collection.

322 Tile with under-glaze printed decoration of an Aesop fable.
Designed by John Moyr Smith.
Dust-pressed, 152 x 152mm.
Minton's China Works, *c.*1885.
Private collection.

323 Tile with a moulded design of a flower in a circular border.
Plastic clay, 152 x 152mm.
Copeland, *c.*1870.
Private collection.

324 Tile with moulded *émaux ombrants* 'photographic' design of *Christ wearing the Crown of Thorns.*
Designed by George Cartlidge.
Dust-pressed, 225 x 152mm.
Sherwin & Cotton, *c.*1905.
City Museum & Art Gallery, Stoke-on-Trent.

325 Tile with under-glaze hand-painted decoration of a female figure with torch.
Plastic clay, 520 x 160mm.
W B Simpson & Sons, *c.*1870.
Private collection.

326 Tile with under-glaze hand-painted landscape.
Dust-pressed, 152 x 152mm.
Maw & Co, *c.*1890.
Private collection.

327 Tile with a moulded design of daffodils painted with glazes.
Dust-pressed, 152 x 152mm.
Henry Richards Tile Co, *c.*1905.
Private collection.

328 Tile with moulded *émaux ombrants* 'photographic' design of children with a horse and cart, entitled *Compliments of the Season.*
Dust-pressed, 113 x 76mm.
Sherwin & Cotton, *c.*1905.
City Museum & Art Gallery, Stoke-on-Trent.

329 Tile with moulded *émaux ombrants* 'photographic' design of a girl playing a mandolin, entitled *A Serenade.*
Designed by George Cartlidge.
Dust-pressed, 113 x 76mm.
Sherwin & Cotton, *c.*1905.
City Museum & Art Gallery, Stoke-on-Trent.

330 Tile with a printed photographic reproduction of *Queen's Apartments, Tutbury, '99.*
Dust-pressed, 150 x 150mm.
Executed by the Photo Decorated Tile Co, on a Pilkington's blank, *c.*1899.
Private collection.

ART NOUVEAU TILES

331 Panel of three Art Nouveau tiles with slip-trailed decoration depicting a flower, berries and leaves.
Plastic clay, each tile 160 x 160mm.
Sherwin & Cotton, *c.*1900.
Private collection.

332 Art Nouveau tile with machine-pressed relief decoration depicting a stylized floral motif.
Dust-pressed, 150 x 150mm.
Maw & Co, *c.*1905.
Private collection.

333 Art Nouveau tile with machine-pressed relief decoration of two flowers in translucent glazes .
Dust-pressed, 150 x 150mm.
Decorative Art Tile Co, c.1900.
Private collection.

334 Art Nouveau tile with machine-pressed relief decoration of three flowers in translucent glazes .
Dust-pressed, 150 x 150mm.
Corn Brothers, c.1900.
Glasgow Museums & Art Galleries.

335 Tile with printed under-glaze decoration with plant and flower designs in the William Morris tradition.
Dust-pressed, 150 x 150mm.
Minton's China Works, c.1882.
Private collection.

336 Art Nouveau tile with machine-pressed relief decoration and a single translucent glaze.
Dust-pressed, 150 x 150mm.
Lea & Boulton, c.1900.
Private collection.

337 Art Nouveau tile with machine-pressed relief decoration and translucent glazes depicting a single floral motif.
Dust-pressed, 150 x 150mm.
Corn Brothers, c.1900.
Private collection.

338 Art Nouveau tile with machine-pressed relief decoration of two flowers in translucent glazes .
Dust-pressed, 150 x 150mm.
T A Simpson & Co, c.1905.
Private collection.

339 Panel of five Art Nouveau tiles with slip-trailed decoration with translucent glazes depicting a floral motif.
Dust-pressed, 150 x 150mm.
Marsden Tile Co, c.1900.
Private collection.

340 Art Nouveau tile with machine-pressed relief decoration with a single translucent glaze.
Dust-pressed, 150 x 150mm.
Alfred Meakin Ltd, c.1905.
Private collection.

341 Two Art Nouveau tiles with slip-trailed decoration and translucent glazes depicting a single flower.
Dust-pressed, each tile 150 x 150mm.
George Woolliscroft & Sons, c.1900.
Private collection.

342 Art Nouveau tile with machine-pressed relief decoration with a single translucent glaze.
Dust-pressed, 150 x 150mm.
Henry Richards Tiles Co, c.1905.
Private collection.

343 Art Nouveau tile with machine-pressed relief decoration with translucent glazes depicting a flower.
Dust-pressed, 150 x 150mm.
T & R Boote, c.1905.
Private collection.

MORRIS & CO TILES

344 Two tiles with on-glaze hand-painted decoration representing the scene of Cinderella leaving the ball. Painted on Dutch tin-glazed blanks.
Plastic clay, each tile 150 x 150mm.
Morris & Co, c.1865.
Private collection.

345 Tile, hand-painted in-glaze in blue with quartered design of flowers and scrolls. Dutch tile in the Arts & Crafts Movement style. Pattern No 50 *Aster* in the catalogue of Thomas Elsley's Portland Metal Works, London (importers).
Plastic clay, 125 x 125mm, c.1880.
Private collection.

346 Tile, hand-painted on-glaze in yellows and oranges with *Oak, Bayleaf and Sunflower* design by William Morris and decorated by Morris & Co on a pre-glazed Dutch blank.
Plastic clay, 125 x 125mm, c.1865.
Private collection.

347 Tile, hand-painted in-glaze in blue after Philip Webb's *Swan* design consisting of 16 squares alternately filled with a swan and a foliate design. Dutch tile made by Ravesteijn of Utrecht, 125 x 125mm, *c.*1885. *Private collection.*

348 Watercolour design by Edward Burne-Jones for Morris & Co for two tiles of Cinderella at the ball, *c.*1860. *Private collection.*

349–350 Two panels hand-painted on-glaze in blues, greens and orange with figures of medieval musicians. Designed by William Morris and painted by Morris & Co. Each tile 152 x 152mm, *c.*1862. *Private collection.*

351 Relief-moulded plaque with a bust of William Morris. Made by the Della Robbia Pottery, Birkenhead, in 1897 as a tribute to Morris after his death in 1896. The cream-coloured relief is set on a blue ground, 450 x 362mm. Della Robbia, 1897. *Williamson Art Gallery, Birkenhead.*

352 Tile, hand-painted under-glaze of *The Lady of Shalott* (after Holman Hunt). Dust-pressed, 102 x 102mm. Minton, Hollins & Co, *c.*1875. *Private collection.*

353 Tile with hand-painted in-glaze decoration of 16 squares filled with alternate sunflower and foliate designs, blue on white. Dutch tile after Morris *Scroll* design, 125 x 125mm, *c.*1885. *Private collection.*

354 Tile, hand-painted in-glaze with a quartered design of chequers and stylized flowers in blue on white. Dutch tile in the Arts & Crafts style. Dust-pressed, 125 x 125mm, *c.*1880. *Private collection.*

355 Two tiles hand-painted on-glaze in greenish-blue with *The Adoration of the Shepherds*. Minton, Hollins & Co blanks, each tile 202 x 202mm, *c.*1875. *Private collection.*

356 Tile, hand-painted in grey-blue with William Morris *Columbine* design. Decorated by Morris & Co on unmarked Dutch plastic clay blanks, 128 x 128mm, *c.*1862. *Private collection.*

357 Panel of eight tiles, hand-painted on-glaze in green and yellow with a repeating design of alternating poppies. Decorated by Morris & Co on unmarked Dutch plastic clay blanks, each tile 127 x 127mm, *c.*1865. *Private collection.*

358 Panel of three tiles, hand-painted under-glaze in purple and green on a white engobe. William Morris design of alternating poppies. Made and decorated by William De Morgan, each tile 130 x 130mm, *c.*1880. *Private collection.*

359 Tile, hand-painted on-glaze in grey-green with a knight on horseback Designed by William Morris and painted by Morris & Co on an unmarked Dutch plastic clay tile, 152 x 152mm, *c.*1865. *Private collection.*

360 Tile, hand-painted on-glaze in grey-blue and yellow with stylized daisies. Designed by William Morris and painted by Morris & Co on an unmarked Dutch plastic clay tile, 152 x 152mm, *c.*1865. *Private collection.*

361 Tile, hand-painted on-glaze in grey-green and yellow with William Morris *Daisy* design of clumps of stylized flowers. Painted by Morris & Co on an unmarked Dutch plastic clay tile, 152 x 152mm, *c.*1865. *Private collection.*

362 Tile, hand-painted in-glaze in blues, greens and yellow with William Morris *Daisy* design of clumps of stylized flowers.
Made and decorated in Holland by Ravesteijn of Utrecht on an unmarked plastic clay tile, 152 x 152mm, *c.*1890.
Private collection.

363 Moulded plaque, majolica glazed in yellows and blues after a design by Edward Burne-Jones.
Della Robbia Pottery, Birkenhead, 210 x 580mm, *c.*1897.
Williamson Art Gallery, Birkenhead.

WILLIAM DE MORGAN TILES

364 Tile, hand-painted under-glaze in greens and blues with William De Morgan *New Persian No 1* design.
Plastic clay, 150 x 150mm.
William De Morgan, *c.*1885.
Private collection.

366 Tile with red lustre hand-painted bird design on a tufted background. Decorated by William De Morgan on a Wedgwood blank, 152 x 152mm, 1870s.
Private collection.

367 Tile, hand-painted under-glaze in blue, green and purple on white with William De Morgan *Bedford Park Anemone*.
Plastic clay, 152 x 152mm.
William De Morgan, *c.*1890.
Private collection.

368 Tile, hand-painted in under-glaze blue with red, amber and silver lustre on a white engobe. William De Morgan design of a *Dodo* bird with foliage.
Plastic clay, 150 x 150mm.
William De Morgan, *c.*1898.
Private collection.

369 Tile, hand-painted under-glaze in greens and purple. William De Morgan design of large leaves with flowers.
Plastic clay, 152 x 152mm.
William De Morgan, *c.*1885.
Private collection.

370 Tile, hand-painted in blues and greens on white. William Morris *Tulip and Trellis* design, decorated by William De Morgan on an Architectural Pottery Co blank, 153 x 153mm, 1870s.
City Museum & Art Gallery, Stoke-on-Trent.

371 Tile, hand-painted in greens on white engobe. William De Morgan design of a galleon in full sail.
Plastic clay, 152 x 152mm.
William De Morgan, 1880s.
Private collection.

372 Panel of nine tiles, hand-painted in red lustre on white with fantastic birds and animals on a foliate ground. Designed and decorated by William De Morgan on commercial dust-pressed blanks, each tile 150 x 150mm.
William De Morgan, 1880s.
Private collection.

373 Tile, hand-painted in green, yellow and light purple on white. Part of the William De Morgan *Pineapple* design.
Plastic clay, 152 x 152mm.
William De Morgan, 1880s.
Private collection.

374 Tile, hand-painted in blue, green and purple on white. William De Morgan design of peacocks.
Plastic clay, 230 x 230mm.
William De Morgan, 1882–88.
Private collection.

375 Two ship tiles, hand-painted in blue, green, purple and brown on white.
Plastic clay, ship tiles each 203 x 203mm.
William De Morgan, *c.*1882.
Private collection.

376 Panel of 16 tiles, hand-painted in blue, green and purple on white, centre section with continuous Iznik design.
Plastic clay, each tile 202 x 202mm.
William De Morgan, c.1888–97.
Private collection.

377 Panel of six tiles, hand-painted in yellow, green and blue on white with a foliate and flower-head design.
Plastic clay, each tile 152 x 152mm.
William De Morgan, c.1890.
Private collection.

378 Panel of six tiles, hand-painted in blue, green, yellow and purple. William De Morgan design of a snake with trees and starry sky behind.
Plastic clay, each tile 152 x 152mm.
William De Morgan, c.1882–88.
Private collection.

TILE DESIGNERS

379–382 Four tiles with under-glaze transfer-printed decoration and hand colouring of the four seasons.
Designed by Kate Greenaway within a Japanesque-style border.
Dust-pressed, each tile 152 x 152mm.
T & R Boote registration mark for 1881 on reverses.
Private collection.

383–385 Three tiles with on-glaze hand-painted decoration of the rhymes *How does my lady's garden grow?*, *Where are you going to my pretty maid?*, and *Mrs Bond*.
Based on designs by Walter Crane.
Dust-pressed, each tile 152 x 152mm.
Painted on Minton, Hollins & Co, blanks, c.1885.
Private collection.

386 Tile with under-glaze printed decoration and hand colouring of children looking through a fence.
Based on a design by Randolph Caldecott.
Dust-pressed, 152 x 152mm.
George Woolliscroft & Son blank, c.1895.
Private collection.

387–389 Panel of three tiles (No 387) with a hand-painted under-glaze design of a horseman in flight and two tiles (Nos 388 and 389) with hand-painted under-glaze decoration depicting a lady on a horse startled by dogs and children cheering a horseman.
Based on a design by Randolph Caldecott (from *The Diverting History of John Gilpin*).
Dust-pressed, each tile 152 x 152mm.
Painted on unmarked Minton's China Works blanks, c.1880.
Private collection.

390 Two tiles from a set of six with under-glaze printed decoration with hand colouring depicting *Greek Musicians*.
Designed by Thomas Allen.
Dust-pressed, each tile 152 x 152mm.
Wedgwood, c.1885.
Private collection.

391 Hexagonal plaque with enamel decoration with a central scene of Sleeping Beauty.
Based on a design by Walter Crane, 370mm in diameter.
French, c.1885.
Private collection.

392 Tile with hand-painted on-glaze decoration depicting a man creeping up on a milkmaid.
Based on a design by Randolph Caldecott.
Dust-pressed, 152 x 152mm.
Painted on an unmarked Minton's China Works blank, c.1880.
Private collection.

393 Teapot stand tile with on-glaze printed decoration with hand colouring depicting a scene from the rhyme *Little Boy Blue*.
Based on a design by Walter Crane.
Plastic clay, 152 x 152mm.
Copeland, 1882.
Private collection.

394 Tile with under-glaze printed design of *The Boaster*.
Based on a design by Walter Crane.
Dust-pressed, 152 x 152mm.
Mosaic Tile Co, Zanesville, Ohio, USA, *c.*1895.
Private collection.

395 Panel of three tiles with hand-painted under-glaze decoration with a scene of horsemen at a crossroads.
Based on a design by Randolph Caldecott (from *The Diverting History of John Gilpin*).
Dust-pressed, each tile 152 x 152mm.
Painted on unmarked Minton's China Works blanks, *c.*1880.
Private collection.

396 Two tiles with printed on-glaze decoration with added hand colour of *Tom Tucker* and *Little Brown Betty*.
Based on designs by Walter Crane.
Dust-pressed, each tile 152 x 152mm.
Maw & Co, *c.*1880.
Private collection.

397–399 Three tiles with under-glaze printed decoration of children within Aesthetic Movement style borders.
Based on designs by Kate Greenaway.
Dust-pressed, each tile 152 x 152mm.
T & R Boote blanks with a registration mark for 1879 on reverse.
Private collection.

400 Tile with under-glaze printed decoration with a scene of *The Doctors and the Dying Man*.
Based on a design by C O Murray.
Dust-pressed, 152 x 152mm.
Maw & Co, *c.*1885.
Private collection.

401 Glass tile with relief-moulded decoration of an elephant's head.
Designed by Hector Guimard.
From Castel Henrietta, 95 x 95mm.
French, *c.*1900.
Private collection.

402 Tile with under-glaze printed decoration with added hand colour of a Japanese fan, landscape and bamboo set against a 'cracked ice' ground.
Dust-pressed, 152 x 152mm.
Sherwin & Cotton, *c.*1885.
Private collection.

403 Tile with under-glaze printed decoration of an oriental fan on which appears a Japanese woman.
Dust-pressed, 152 x 152mm.
Minton's China Works, *c.*1885.
Private collection.

404 Tile with under-glaze printed decoration of oriental-style branches.
Dust-pressed, 152 x 152mm.
Minton's China Works, *c.*1885.
Private collection.

405 Tile with under-glaze printed decoration of oriental foliage.
Dust-pressed, 152 x 152mm.
Webb's Tileries, Worcester, with a registration mark for 1884 on reverse.
Private collection.

406 Four tiles with under-glaze printed decoration of sheep, cows and horses.
Designed by William Wise.
Dust-pressed, each tile 152 x 152mm.
Minton's China Works, *c.*1885.
Private collection.

407 Tile, slip-trailed carpenter design.
Designed by C F A Voysey.
Plastic clay, 125 x 125mm.
Possibly made by Medmenham tiles, Marlow, Buckinghamshire, *c.*1899.
Private collection.

408 Tile with under-glaze printed decoration of children by a stile.
Based on illustrations in the children's magazine *The Rosebud*.
Dust-pressed, 152 x 152mm. Unmarked.
Private collection.

409 Panel of six tiles with machine-pressed line relief decoration with a repeating design of fish and waterlilies.
Designed by C F A Voysey.
Dust-pressed, each tile 152 x 152mm.
Pilkington, *c.*1903.
Private collection.

410 Two tiles with slip-trailed decoration covered with a green translucent glaze depicting two female heads in Art Nouveau style, signed 'MH'. The tile on the left is based on a watercolour by Eleanor Fortescue Brickdale with the title *Chance*, an illustration of which appeared in *The Studio*, Vol 23, 1901.
Dust-pressed, each tile 150 x 150mm.
J & W Wade (Flaxman Tile Works), *c*.1901.
Private collection.

411 Teapot stand with relief-moulded decoration under a glaze with a 'self portrait' of its designer C F A Voysey.
Dust-pressed, 152 x 152mm.
J C Edwards, Ruabon, North Wales, *c*.1900.
Private collection.

412 Three tiles with relief-moulded decoration of a bird and foliage.
Designed by C F A Voysey.
Dust-pressed, 152 x 152mm.
Pilkington, *c*.1903.
Private collection.

413 Tile with stencilled on-glaze lustre decoration with a 'self portrait' of its designer C F A Voysey.
Dust-pressed, 152 x 152mm.
J C Edwards, Ruabon, North Wales, *c*.1890.
Private collection.

414 Six tiles with relief-moulded decoration of floral and foliate design under various coloured glazes.
Designed by Lewis F Day.
Dust-pressed, each tile 152 x 152mm.
Pilkington, *c*.1905.
Private collection.

415 Panel of 16 tiles with tube-lined decoration of a repeating motif of a bird in a cherry tree.
Designed by C F A Voysey.
Dust-pressed, each tile 152 x 152mm.
Maw & Co, *c*.1900.
Private collection

416 Panel of eight tiles with hand-painted decoration with a 'Persian' design of swirling leaves and flowers. A prize-winning panel designed by Sidney Denny Marsden, each tile 152 x 152mm.
Marsden Tiles, 1897.
Private collection.

417 Panel of 40 tiles, alternate tiles depicting nursery rhymes. Hand-painted in-glaze in bright colours.
Designed by Dora Batty.
Pressed plastic clay, each tile 105 x 105mm.
Carter, Stabler & Adams, *c*.1935.
Private collection.

TILES IN USE

418 Art Nouveau panel with tube-lined decoration.
Plastic clay, each square tile 250 x 250mm.
Doulton & Co, *c*.1900.
From the public house *The Locomotive*, Hull (demolished 1974).
Private collection.

419 Panel entitled *Ladies Papers*. Stencilled and hand-painted in various colours, 603 x 422mm overall.
Designed for W H Smith & Son.
Carter & Co, Poole, *c*.1930.
Private collection.

420 Panel of three tiles depicting three male heads, painted over-glaze in strong colours with heavy black outlines.
Designed by W J Neatby for Harrods, London.
Plastic clay.
Possibly Doulton & Co, Lambeth, *c*.1900.
Private collection.

421 Panel of 15 tiles with slip-trailed decoration and coloured glazes.
Dust-pressed.
Designed for the firm Panther Ltd by the tile decorator J Duncan Ltd of Glasgow, *c*.1925.
Glasgow Museums & Art Galleries.

422 Panel of 18 tiles with tube-lined decoration depicting a lady angler in Classical dress.
Dust-pressed tiles
Designed for a fish shop and decorated by J Duncan Ltd of Glasgow, *c*.1925.
Glasgow Museums & Art Galleries.

423 Tiled fireplace with transfer-printed tiles as illustrated in Maw & Co's catalogue of *c*.1885. The figurative tiles depict Japanese ladies in traditional dress in different oriental settings.
Designed by Owen Gibbons.
Originally fitted inside Huddersfield Town Hall. [*See also* No 227.]
Kirklees Museums & Galleries.

424 Glazed ceramic paraffin stove with moulded decoration of palmettes and acanthus leaf scrolls. It has a detachable cover with leaded light panels, the paraffin heater sits inside.
Burmantofts, *c*.1890.
Leeds City Museums.

425 Marble-topped washstand with a splash-back of green Art Nouveau tiles.
Dust-pressed tiles
Maker not known, *c*.1905.
Private collection.

426 Washstand with a tiled top and a large splash-back of William De Morgan tiles with flowers painted in purple, green and yellow, *c*.1890.
Private collection.

427 Hall-stand with a mirror below which is a set of four tiles from a series of 12 depicting the *Idylls of the Kings*.
Designed by John Moyr Smith.
Minton's China Works, *c*.1880.
Private collection.

428 Mirror with 12 tiles in the surround depicting the *Spirits of the Flowers*.
Designed by John Moyr Smith.
Minton's China Works, *c*.1880.
Private collection.

429 Bamboo plant stand inset with tiles depicting Japanese-style birds in flight.
Designed by Christopher Dresser.
Minton's China Works, *c*.1880.
Private collection.

EUROPEAN TILES

430 Tile with brown-printed under-glaze decoration of a central abstract design with corner motifs.
Dust-pressed, 151 x 151mm.
Regout, Maastricht, Holland, *c*.1890.
Private collection.

431 Tile with stencilled under-glaze decoration in green, brown and black, of a Jugendstil flower with leaves.
Dust-pressed.
De Porceleyne Fles (Joost Thooft & Labouchere), Delft, Holland, *c*.1900.
Private collection.

432 Tile with pseudo-mosaic inlaid design in green, red, buff and white.
Dust-pressed, 168 x 166mm.
Villeroy & Boch, Germany, *c*.1885.
Private collection.

433 Tile with dark blue printed under-glaze decoration of a moonlit scene with figures in a boat on a lake within an Art Nouveau border.
Dust-pressed, 151 x 75mm.
Les Majoliques de Hasselt, Belgium, *c*.1900.
Private collection.

434 Tile with red-printed under-glaze decoration of an Art Nouveau motif.
Dust-pressed, 150 x 75mm.
Les Majoliques de Hasselt, Belgium.
Private collection.

435 Tile with brown-printed under-glaze decoration of a girl sitting on a doorstep with a cat and a bird on a string.
Dust-pressed, 150 x 150mm.
French, *c*.1885.
Private collection.

436 Tile with black-printed under-glaze decoration with an abstract motif.
Dust-pressed, 150 x 150mm.
French, *c*.1890.
Private collection.

437 Tile with blue-green under-glaze transfer-printed decoration of a star-like central motif.
Dust-pressed, 145 x 145mm.
Villeroy & Boch, Germany, *c*.1890.
Private collection

438 Tile with machine-pressed relief decoration of a water-lily with translucent glazes in green and blue.
Dust-pressed, 150 x 150mm.
Norddeutsche Steingutfabrik, Grohn bei Bremen, Germany, *c*.1910.
Private collection.

439 Tile with machine-pressed relief decoration of a Jugendstil motif with grey and dark green translucent glazes.
Dust-pressed, 152 x 152mm.
Boizenburger Wandplattenfabrik, Germany, *c*.1925.
Private collection.

440 Tile with stencilled under-glaze decoration in black, brown and green, of a leaf design with palmette motifs.
Dust-pressed, 145 x 145mm.
Villeroy & Boch, Germany, *c*.1890.
Private collection.

441 Tile with a brown under-glaze printed decoration of a star-like central motif.
Dust-pressed, 150 x 150mm.
Possibly Wessel's Wandplatten Fabrik, Bonn, Germany, *c*.1890.
Private collection.

442 Unglazed encaustic floor tile inlaid with blue, red, yellow, green and shades of brown with a large central monogram.
Dust-pressed, 168 x 168mm.
Villeroy & Boch, Germany, *c*.1885.
Private collection.

443 Four tiles with machine-pressed relief designs with green, red and blue translucent glazes depicting Dutch scenes.
Dust-pressed, each tile 150 x 150mm.
Norddeutsche Steingutfabrik, Grohn bei Bremen, Germany, *c*.1925.
Private collection.

444 Tile with machine-pressed relief decoration of a triangular Art Deco motif with green and deep red translucent glazes.
Dust-pressed, 150 x 150mm.
Servais Werke A G Ehrang, Germany, *c*.1920.
Private collection.

445 Tile with machine-pressed relief decoration with dark blue and yellow decoration depicting two interlocking wreaths with ribbons.
Dust-pressed, 150 x 150mm.
Norddeutsche Steingutfabrik, Grohn bei Bremen, Germany, *c*.1925.
Private collection.

446 Tile with dry-cord technique decoration (*cuerda seca*) and richly coloured opaque glazes in turquoise, yellow, green, red and blue depicting an exotic bird amid bamboo.
Dust-pressed, 200 x 200mm.
L M Montereau, Creil, France, *c*.1865.
Private collection.

447 Tile painted with coloured slips (barbotine) covered with a clear transparent glaze depicting a coastal scene with fishing boats.
Dust-pressed, 203 x 203mm.
Boulenger, Auneuil, France, 1900.
Private collection.

448 Tile with dry-cord technique decoration (*cuerda seca*) with coloured glazes in turquoise and red of flowers and leaves.
Plastic clay, 205 x 205mm.
Longwy Faience Factory, Longwy, France, early-19th century.
Private collection.

449 Tile with dry-cord technique decoration (*cuerda seca*) with richly coloured opaque glazes in blue, green, pink and yellow, depicting a flower and an insect within a cross-shaped form.
Dust-pressed, 200 x 200mm.
J Loebnitz, Paris, France, *c*.1885.
Private collection.

450 Unglazed encaustic tile with black inlay with a medieval-style leaf motif.
Plastic clay, 137 x 137mm.
Boulenger, Auneuil, France, *c*.1880.
Private collection.

451 Unglazed encaustic tile with red and black inlay with a vine leaf border.
Plastic clay, 139 x 139mm.
Boulenger, Auneuil, France, *c*.1880.
Private collection.

452 Unglazed encaustic tile with red, blue, orange and brown inlay depicting a stylized floral motif.
Dust-pressed, 144 x 145mm.
Boch Freres, Maubeuge, Northern France, *c*.1890.
Private collection.

453 Unglazed encaustic tile with green, blue, yellow and grey inlay making a Moorish motif.
Dust-pressed, 140 x 140mm.
Octave Colozier, Beauvais, France, *c*.1910.
Private collection.

454 Unglazed encaustic tile with dark brown, blue and white inlay with stylized chestnut blossom and leaves.
Dust-pressed, 125 x 125mm.
Douzies, Maubeuge, France, *c*.1900.
Private collection.

455 Unglazed encaustic tile with blue, dark and light grey inlay with a stylized central motif of leaves within a geometric design.
Dust-pressed, 150 x 150mm.
Douzies, Maubeuge, France, *c*.1900.
Private collection.

456 Two *cuenca* tiles with a circular Moorish pattern painted in green, red and blue with white line work.
Dust-pressed, each tile 275 x 137mm.
Mensaque Rodriguez, Seville, Spain, *c*.1900.
The development of the *cuenca* technique goes back to the late-15th and early-16th centuries as can be seen in the 16th century Spanish *cuenca* tiles illustrated under Nos 457 and 458.
Private collection.

457 Two *cuenca* tiles from the ceiling of a church in Seville with a circular wreath painted with green and orange-brown glazes.
Plastic clay, each tile 270 x 130mm.
Spanish, *c*.1560.
Private collection.

458 Panel of four *cuenca* tiles painted with green glazes and gold lustre of a circular motif set within an octagon.
Plastic clay, each tile 140 x 140mm.
Spanish, *c*.1500.
Private collection.

20TH CENTURY BRITISH TILES

459 Stoneware tile with hand-painted under-glaze decoration of a blackthorn.
Plastic clay, 152 x 152mm.
Made by Bernard Leach at St Ives Pottery, Cornwall, *c*.1930.
Private collection.

460 Tile, hand-painted in green, red and ochre with in-glaze decoration of a Dutch girl. From the *Coloured Dutch* series designed by Joseph Roelants.
Pressed plastic clay, 152 x 152mm.
Carter, Stabler & Adams, *c*.1920.
Private collection.

461 Tile, stencilled under-glaze with a ploughing scene in green, blue, orange and black.
Henry Richards dust-pressed blank, 152 x 152mm. From a series of farming scenes decorated by Dunsmore Tiles, *c*.1930.
Private collection.

462 Stoneware tile, hand-painted in-glaze with a Korean landscape in blue-black on a greyish buff ground. Plastic clay, 100 x 100mm. Made by Bernard Leach at St Ives Pottery, Cornwall, c.1930, and signed on the face with his 'BL' monogram. Impressed St Ives mark on the reverse. *Private collection.*

463 Tile, hand-painted in-glaze of a cheeky dog, black outline with touches of tan on an off-white ground. From the *Dogs* series designed by Cecil Aldin, signed on face. Pressed plastic clay, 127 x 127mm. Carter, Stabler & Adams, c.1935. *Private collection.*

464 Tile, with design in coloured glazes over a black outline, Dutch boy and girl in greens, blue, red, orange and grey. Dust-pressed tile, 152 x 152mm. Henry Richards, c.1920. *Jackfield Tile Museum.*

465 Three tiles, tube-lined with eggshell glazes in Art Deco designs, greys, greens, reds and some gold highlights. Dust-pressed, each tile 102 x 102mm. Maw & Co, c.1930–40. *Jackfield Tile Museum.*

466 Tile, tube-lined with eggshell glazes of a ship in blue and brown. Designed by Edmund Kent. Dust-pressed, 102 x 102mm. Pilkington, c.1930. *Private collection.*

467 Tile, moulded outline and eggshell glazes in brown, green and grey of a galleon Dust-pressed, 102 x 102mm. Maker not known, c.1930. *Private collection.*

468 Tile, hand-painted under-glaze with a female head in brown. Plastic clay, 105 x 105mm. Possibly Carter, Stabler & Adams, c.1920. *Private collection.*

469 Plaque, moulded and glazed with eggshell glazes in dark green and brown with white and pink, depicting a lion rampant and the flowers of the nations. Inscribed 'CORONATION 1937'. Dark red plastic clay, 157 x 210mm. Malkin Tiles, 1937. *Private collection.*

470 Tile, tube-lined with eggshell glazes in an Art Deco sun-ray design in orange and red. Dust-pressed, 102 x 102mm. Maw & Co, c.1935. *Jackfield Tile Museum.*

471 Tile, tube-lined with eggshell glazes of a diagonal design of a ship with a black hull and red sails. Dust-pressed, 102 x 102mm. Maw & Co, c.1935. *Jackfield Tile Museum.*

472 Tile, hand-painted under-glaze with stylized birds and a flower in blues, greens and reds. *Birds and Flowers* series No BF4. Designed by Rosalind Ord and probably painted by Thea Bridges. Decorated by Packard & Ord on a James Plant & Son dust-pressed blank, 100 x 100mm, 1937–38. *Private collection.*

473 Tile, hand-painted in glaze with *Little Bo-Peep* from the *Nursery Rhymes* series in green, blue, pink and black. Designed by Dora Batty Pressed plastic clay, 152 x 152mm. Carter, Stabler & Adams, c.1930. *Private collection.*

474 Tile, hand-painted in-glaze with a further clear glaze over a *Flying Horseman* design in green and brown. Special commission painted by Rosalind Ord and signed 'RO' on the reverse. Packard & Ord decoration on a Carter pressed plastic clay blank, 152 x 152mm, c.1933. *Private collection.*

475 Tile, hand-painted in-glaze with a design of gambolling sheep in a leafy bower in browns and greens.
Designed by Sylvia Packard, painted by Rosalind Ord and signed 'RO' on bottom edge. *Pastoral* series No P5.
Decorated by Packard & Ord on a Rhodes Tile Co dust-pressed blank, 152 x 152mm, *c*.1936.
Private collection.

476 Four-relief moulded tiles with decoration symbolic of London and the London Underground system with a creamy semi-matt glaze.
Designed by Harold Stabler for the refurbishment of the London Underground and signed 'S' on the face.
Pressed plastic clay, each tile 152 x 152mm.
Carter, Stabler & Adams, *c*.1938–39.
City Museum & Art Gallery, Stoke-on-Trent.

477 Four tiles depicting characters from *Alice in Wonderland*. Stencilled/printed in browns, greens, blues, reds, on a white ground.
From designs by C F A Voysey from the original Tenniel edition.
Decorated by Dunsmore Tiles on Minton dust-pressed blanks, each tile 152 x 152mm, *c*.1930.
Private collection.

478 Tile with stencilled/printed decoration in black, green, orange and blue on a mottled white ground.
From the same series as No 477.
Dunsmore decoration on a Minton dust-pressed blank, 126 x 126mm, *c*.1930.
Private collection.

479 Tile with hand-painted in-glaze decoration depicting *Little Nell and Grandfather* from the *Small Dickens* series No SDK19, in greens and browns, on a cream ground.
Decorated by Packard & Ord on an H & G Thynne dust-pressed blank, 100 x 100mm, 1950.
Private collection.

480 Three tiles with on-glaze screen-printed decoration with Moorish-style designs by Reginald Till.
Dust-pressed, each tile 102 x 102mm, 1967–68.
Private collection

481 Tile with on-glaze screen-printed decoration.
Designed by Reginald Till.
Dust-pressed, 150 x 150mm.
Carter & Co, 1962.
Private collection.

482 Tile with hand-painted decoration.
Dust-pressed, 100 x 100mm, *c*.1950.
Private collection.

483 Tile with hand-painted under-glaze decoration in green, brown and yellow on white with a *London Cries* scene.
Unknown decorator on a Carter blank, 152 x 152mm, 1954.
Private collection.

484 Tile, colour chart with silk-screen printed colours, white, black, browns, greys and greens etc.
Dust-pressed, 152 x 152mm.
Maw & Co, 1960s.
Jackfield Tile Museum.

485 Tile with on-glaze screen-printed decoration of an abstract design.
Dust-pressed, 150 x 150mm.
Maw & Co, 1964.
Jackfield Tile Museum.

486 Tile with litho-printed design for Festival of Britain, 1951. Black outline with blue on white.
Dust-pressed, 152 x 152mm.
H & G Thynne, 1951.
Private collection.

487 Tile with hand-painted and sgraffito decoration of a river scene with a footbridge.
Designed and executed by Alan Caiger-Smith, signed with 'CS' monogram.
Vitrified dust-pressed body.
George Woolliscroft blank, 1976.
Private collection.

488 Tile with on-glaze printed half-tone photographic transfer of a tractor shifting hay.
Dust-pressed, 150 x 150mm.
H & R Johnson,1967.
Glastone Pottery Museum.

489 Tile with on-glaze screen-printed decoration depicting a cockerel.
Designed by Reginald Till, 1952.
Dust-pressed, 150 x 150mm.
Private collection.

490 Tile with hand-painted and sgraffito decoration depicting a cockerel in blues and greens on a blue ground over a red body.
Designed and executed by Alan Caiger-Smith, signed with 'CS' monogram.
Vitrified dust-pressed body.
Carter blank, 1971.
Private collection.

491 Four tiles screen-printed over-glaze in browns, greens, orange, black and purple, symbolic of the four seasons.
Designed by John Piper and made at the Fulham Pottery, London, in a limited edition of 150.
Plastic clay, 150 x 150mm, 1983.
Private collection.

CONTEMPORARY TILES

492 Border tile of a hand-painted fish.
Designed by Jonathan Waights, 1991.
Dust-pressed blank, 150 x 75mm.
Art on Tiles, London.

493 Border tile of a hand-painted stylized leaf and flower.
Designed by Jonathan Waights, 1991.
Dust-pressed blank, 150 x 75mm.
Art on Tiles, London.

494 Abstract 'squares' design tile, part of a set of nine. Transparent coloured glazes silk-screen printed by hand and over-printed to produce subtle colours.
Designed by Ann Clark, 1990.
Dust-pressed, each tile 150 x 150mm.
Kenneth Clark Ceramics, Lewes, Sussex.

495 Two tiles from a set of six individual designs depicting landscapes, animals, people, etc. The 'picture' is built up by several applications of hand-sprayed glaze. The tile is fired and sgraffito decoration is applied at each stage.
Designed and made by Ann Clark, early-1980s.
Dust-pressed, each tile 150 x 150mm.
Kenneth Clark Ceramics, Lewes, Sussex.

496 *Robin on a Twig, Christmas 1987.* Each year Paul Henry designs and makes a special Christmas tile. This one, for 1987, he not only designed but also made the mould from which it was slip-cast. The 'Victorian' green and crazed glaze was specially developed for him by Blythe Colours Ltd of Cresswell, Stoke-on-Trent, 150 x 150mm
Paul Henry, London.

497 Pilkington transfer-printed centenary tile (1891–1991) with calendar for 1991.
Dust-pressed, 150 x 150mm.
Pilkington, 1991.
Pilkington's Tiles Ltd, Clifton Junction, Manchester.

498 Tile panel depicting two parrots in a cage with a border of stylized foliage, hand-painted in under-glaze colours .
Designed by Jonathan Waights, 1990.
Dust-pressed blanks, 620 x 460mm overall.
Art on Tiles, London.

499 Border tile of a hand-painted ivy leaf.
Designed by Jonathan Waights, 1991.
Dust-pressed blank, 150 x 75mm.
Art on Tiles, London.

500 Siamese cat tile, hand-painted in under-glaze colours.
Designed by Maisie Seneshal, late-1960s.
Dust-pressed blank, 105 x 105mm.
Private collection.

501 Panel of six tiles of an urn of fruit, the urn bearing a face, the handles forming ears and ear-rings. Hand-painted in tin-glaze and oxide colours.
Designed by Gesine Mahoney, 1991.
Dust-pressed, 450 x 300mm overall.
Gesine Mahoney, St Columb Minor, Newquay, Cornwall

502 Glazed transfer-printed wall tile from the *Victoria* range, part of the *Royal Lancastrian* collection.
Dust-pressed, 150 x 150mm.
Pilkington, 1991.
Pilkington's Tiles Ltd, Clifton Junction, Manchester.

503 Garlanded fish tile, a copy of a 1930s Italian design, screen-printed and hand-coloured under-glaze.
Designed by John Burgess, 1990
Dust-pressed, 150 x 150mm.
John Burgess Tiles, Jackfield, Shropshire.

504 Arabesque design, hand-painted on tin-glaze.
Dust-pressed blank, 141 x 141mm.
Viuva Lamego, Lisbon, Portugal, 1990.
Private collection.

505 Floor tile from the *Cambrian Classic* range with impressed design and black infill glaze
Red plastic clay, 95 x 95mm.
Dennis Ruabon, 1990.
Dennis Ruabon Ltd, Wrexham, Clwyd, Wales.

506 Wall tile from the *Fettecento* range, majolica colours on a crackle glaze background, imported from Southern Italy, 1991, 150 x 150mm.
Fired Earth Tiles plc, Adderbury, Oxfordshire.

507 Saracen warrior, reproduction of original delft saracen tiles made between 1610 and 1630, metal oxides on tin-glaze.
Made by Piet Jonker, Amsterdam, 1990, 130 x 130mm.
[See also No 45.]
Fired Earth Tiles plc, Adderbury, Oxfordshire.

508 Relief bee tile with a border of fruit and flowers. *Harvest* range, slip-cast and hand-painted with oxides over tin-glaze.
Designed and made by Kim Donaldson, 1990.
Bee tile 110 x 101mm, corners 60 x 60mm, border strips 110 x 60mm.
Fired Earth Tiles plc, Adderbury, Oxfordshire.

509 Arabesque tile, part of a panel, rich under-glaze colours, imported from Turkey, 1990, 200 x 200mm.
Fired Earth Tiles plc, Adderbury, Oxfordshire.

510 Minstrel tile, hand-painted on red plastic clay body, imported from Moustier, France, 1990, 110 x 110mm.
Fired Earth Tiles plc, Adderbury, Oxfordshire.

511 Four tiles suitable for floors or walls from the *Cosmos* range. Hand-painted using tin-glaze and oxide colours.
Designed by Stephen Cocker, 1991.
Plastic clay, 75 x 75mm.
Stephen Cocker, Bedale, North Yorkshire.

512 Three *Celestial* relief tiles, white earthenware painted with tin-glazes and lustres.
Designed by Carlo Briscoe, 1991.
Slip-cast, each tile 67 x 67mm.
Carlo Briscoe, London.

513 Panel of Persian-inspired star and cross tiles bearing various figurative subjects in white earthenware. Hand-painted in oxides under an alkaline glaze.
Designed by Carlo Briscoe, 1991.
Slip-cast, 575 x 390mm overall.
Carlo Briscoe, London.

514 Medieval-style encaustic tile bearing a lurching hound design. Hand-pressed plastic clay inlaid with slip, glazed and then fired in a wood-fired kiln.
Made by Diana Hall, 1991,
105 x 105mm.
Diana Hall, Iford, Sussex.

515 Encaustic tile with a crouching hare amidst foliage, reworked from a 14th century design found at Notley Abbey, Buckinghamshire.
Sold as a 'souvenir' at the Royal Academy of Arts *Age of Chivalry* exhibition.
Made by Diana Hall, 1987,
110x 110mm.
Diana Hall, Iford, Sussex.

516 Hand-moulded tile with bronze lustre fish on a blue background.
Designed and made by Edward Dunn, 1991, 220 x 252mm.
Edward Dunn, Reptile Tiles & Ceramics, London.

517 Four tiles suitable for floors or walls from the *Cosmos* range. Hand-painted using tin-glaze and oxide colours.
Designed by Stephen Cocker, 1991.
Plastic clay, 150 x 150mm.
Stephen Cocker, Bedale, North Yorkshire.

518 Rainbow panel of 100 tiles in various geometric designs, silk-screen printed by hand with hand-sprayed, transparent-coloured glazes of browns through yellows, greens, blues, mauves and pinks.
Designed by Ann Clark, Simon Clark and Alexander Fostiropoulos during the early 1980s.
Dust-pressed blanks, each 100 x 100mm.
Kenneth Clark Ceramics, Lewes, Sussex.

519 *Fantasy Rainforest*, part of a 200-tile panel of exuberant design using many colours and glaze interactions.
Designed and painted by Jan O'Highway, Southsea, Portsmouth.
Dust-pressed blanks, each 152 x 152mm.
Private collection.

520 Panel of 24 abstract and geometric single tile designs, decorated in a wide range of colours with hand-trailed transparent glazes on white-glazed tile.
Designed by Ann Clark.
Dust-pressed blanks, each 150 x 150mm
Kenneth Clark Ceramics, Lewes, Sussex.

521 Six tiles stencilled under-glaze on coloured engobes with designs by Salvador Dali in reds, greens, brown, yellows, blues, etc.
Limited edition by Mikana A G, Spain, each tile 200 x 200mm, 1954.
Private collection.

522 Panel of nine tiles depicting a crouching male figure, hand-painted using dry cord technique (*cuerda seca*).
Designed by Bronwyn Williams-Ellis, 1988.
Dust-pressed blanks, each 150 x 150mm.
Bronwyn Williams-Ellis, Bath, Avon.

523 Panel of 12 tiles depicting a copper pot full of gooseberries against a black background, hand-painted with over-glaze colours.
Designed by Jonathan Waights, 1990.
Dust-pressed blanks, 620 x 420mm overall.
Art on Tiles, London.

524 Tile panel depicting centrally positioned tree with birds beneath, hand-decorated using tube-lining with hand-trailed and sprayed coloured glazes of emerald green, pale greens, browns and blues.
Designed by Ann Clark, 1991.
Dust-pressed blanks 708 x 598mm overall.
Kenneth Clark Ceramics, Lewes, Sussex.